P9-CMO-215

Dr. Chris Thurman's significant book *The Lies We Believe* will shake you up, knock you down, stand you up straight and challenge the very heart of your soul. It is a hard-hitting, eye-opening book. It is a must for every Christian—easy reading and great stuff. A helpful, provocative and meaningful book for all believers.

Dr. Kevin Leman
Clinical psychologist
Author of *Unlocking the Secrets of Your Childhood Memories* and *The Birth Order Book*

We're confronted by lies everyday—our culture lies to us, our religious teachers lie to us, we even lie to ourselves. Dr. Thurman not only does an outstanding job in identifying and examining these lies, he gives us sound and practical steps for facing the truth and being set free by the truth. It is a must-read book for everyone.

Anyone in the business of helping people will benefit from Dr. Thurman's insightful analysis of the lies we let govern our lives, and his biblical and practical steps for how the truth can really set us free.

Dr. David Stoop
Clinical psychologist
Author of *Living with a Perfectionist*

The
Lies
We
Believe

CHRIS THURMAN

THE LIES WE BELIEVE

THOMAS NELSON PUBLISHERS

NASHVILLE

Published in Nashville, Tennessee, by Thomas Nelson, Inc. and distributed
in Canada by Lawson Falle, Ltd., Cambridge, Ontario.

Printed in the United States of America.

Unless otherwise noted, the Bible version used in this publication is THE
NEW KING JAMES VERSION of the Bible. Copyright © 1979, 1980, 1982,
Thomas Nelson, Inc., Publishers.

Scripture Verses noted NIV are from the Holy Bible: New International
Version. Copyright © 1978 by the New York International Bible Society.
Used by permission of Zondervan Bible Publishers.

Library of Congress Cataloging-in-Publication Data

Thurman, Chris.
    The lies we believe / Chris Thurman.
      p.   cm.
    Bibliography: p.
    ISBN 0-8407-3498-0
    1. Christian life—1960-   2. Conduct of life. 3. Errors, Popular.
I. Title.
BV4501.2.T523   1989
248.4—dc19   88-37585
                                     CIP

2 3 4 5 6 7 8 9 10 - 96 95 94 93 92 91 90 89

With great love and appreciation,
this book is dedicated
to my wife, Holly.

Contents

Acknowledgments   xi
Foreword   xv

PART ONE: LIVING WITH LIES

1. THE TRUTH ABOUT THE LIES
   WE BELIEVE   19

PART TWO: THE LIES WE BELIEVE

2. SELF-LIES   35

   "I Must Be Perfect"
   "I Must Have Everyone's Love and
       Approval"
   "It Is Easier to Avoid Problems Than
       to Face Them"
   "I Can't Be Happy Unless Things
       Go My Way"
   "It's Somebody Else's Fault"

3. WORLDY LIES   59

   "You Can Have It All"
   "You Are Only As Good As What
       You Do"

"Life Should be Easy"
"Life Should Be Fair"
"Don't Wait"
"People Are Basically Good"

4. MARITAL LIES   85

"It's All Your Fault"
"If It Takes Hard Work, We Must
    Not Be Right for Each Other"
"You Can and Should Meet All My
    Needs"
"You Owe Me"
"I Shouldn't Have to Change"
"You Should Be Like Me"

5. DISTORTION LIES   109

"A Mountain out of a Molehill"
"Taking Everything Personally"
"Black/White"
"Missing the Forest for the Trees"
"History Always Repeats Itself"
"Don't Confuse Me with the Facts"

6. RELIGIOUS LIES   133

"God's Love Must Be Earned"
"God Hates the Sin and Sinner"
"Because I'm a Christian, God Will
    Protect Me from Pain and
    Suffering"
"All My Problems Are Caused by
    My Sins"
"It Is My Christian Duty to Meet All
    the Needs of Others"
"A Good Christian Doesn't Feel
    Angry, Anxious, or Depressed"

"God Can't Use Me Unless I'm
Spiritually Strong"

PART THREE: LIVING WITH TRUTH

7. THE TRUTH ABOUT TRUTH   163
8. THE TRUTH ABOUT CHANGE   177

APPENDICES

Appendix A: Secular and Theological Truths
for Defeating Lies   191
Appendix B: Secular and Theological
Teachings on the Importance
of the Mind for Healthy
Living   199
Appendix C: Reading List   203

Notes   205

Acknowledgments

As I write these words of acknowledgment, two and a half years have passed since I began writing "The Lies We Believe." It has been a very enjoyable process and a sometimes painful one. There are many people to thank for their support and encouragement.

I owe my deepest thanks to my wife, Holly. She was always there with a word of encouragement when I needed it most, never failing in her efforts to let me know she believed in what I had to say. On many nights when I needed to return to the clinic and work into the early morning hours on the book, she sacrificially let me go, often waiting up until I would drag in at one or two o'clock in the morning to see how I was doing. She has suffered through the rewrites, title changes, editorial delays, and everything else a book goes through before it reaches the reader's hands. She is, as Proverbs describes, a wife of noble character worth far more than rubies. Her loving influence is present throughout this book.

My sincere thanks go to the wonderful staff at Thomas Nelson Publishers. They are professional through and through. They helped me to feel valued and important even though this is my first book. Special thanks to Janet Thoma, who acquired my book for Thomas Nelson. She treated my book as if it were one of her own children, watching out for it, nursing it along, making sure it was being properly taken care of. Special thanks also to Lynda Stephenson, who edited the manuscript. She worked very hard and did a great job. Finally, thanks to Susan Salmon for her efforts in getting the manuscript ready to go to press. She could not have been more helpful or kind.

Many friends and colleagues read and critiqued the manuscript. I appreciate their hard work and input more than they know. Thanks to: Dr. Fred Lopez, William Lamb, Henry Oursler, Dr. Les Carter, Dr. Shed Mc-Williams, Dr. David Nicholson, John Patredis, Dr. Horace Lukens, and Steve Thurman. Thanks also to Dr. M. Scott Peck for reviewing my book. While he did not always agree with my ideas, he provided valuable input and was quite encouraging.

I owe a debt of gratitude to colleagues in the field of cognitive therapy whom I do not know personally: Dr. Albert Ellis (whose writings on irrational beliefs form the basis of Chapter Two), Dr. Aaron Beck and Dr. David Burns (whose writings on cognitive distortions form the basis of Chapter Five), Dr. William Backus, and Dr. David Stoop. Each has made a significant contribution to helping us understand the destructive role that "faulty" thinking plays in our lives, and my book truly stands on their shoulders.

I also owe many thanks to a group of colleagues I know very well, the professional and support staff at the Minirth-Meier Clinic. I have enjoyed working with them for the past four years and appreciate being able to call the clinic my professional home. A heartfelt thanks to Frank Minirth, M.D., and Paul Meier, M.D., for their kind support since I joined the clinic. Also a special thank you to Don Hawkins, Th.M., for the many ways he has encouraged me, especially in the writing of this book. His support has meant a great deal.

Finally, I am especially indebted to the "Texoma boys," Dr. Ben Albritton, Ed Lucas, Richard Maas, and Dr. David Nicholson. They have been among the most significant healing influences in my life.

In closing, I thank God for loving me no matter what and for His help in dealing with the lies that have plagued my own life. God is truth, and truth sets us free. I am thankful for the truth and freedom I have found in Him.

Chris Thurman, Ph.D.
Minirth-Meier Clinic
Richardson, Texas
December, 1988

Foreword

Do we actually believe lies? We certainly do! On an intellectual and, most certainly, on an emotional level, we all wrestle with lies; and our response to them may very well determine our happiness or sadness, peace or worry, and mental health or mental disorders.

Paul Meier and I asked Chris Thurman to conduct small group sessions at our hospital in Dallas on how to counteract the lies we believe with the truth. Of everything we've done in the last year, this was the most important to our patients.

I believe that Chris has transferred much insight from those sessions to these pages. In his unique and gentle way, he helps us weave our way through the lies in our minds. He guides us with the zeal of a youth and the wisdom of an elder.

I pray that Christians can be restored to the joy of their salvation through the common sense in this book.

Frank Minirth, M.D.
Minirth-Meier Clinic
Richardson, Texas

PART ONE

LIVING
WITH
LIES

1.

The Truth About the Lies We Believe

Almost all our misfortunes in life
come from the wrong notions we have
about the things that happen to us.

Marie Stendhal

anet sat nervously on the edge of my office couch, unsure where to begin. This was her first session with me. She'd never visited a psychologist before, and I could see she was feeling embarrassed. The depression she'd felt for several months was getting worse, or she'd probably never have decided to come at all.

Fidgeting nervously, she finally said, "Dr. Thurman, I don't really know where to begin. It's just that I've felt so unhappy lately. Everything seems to be going wrong in my life."

"Why don't you start with what is bothering you the most?" I suggested.

She shook her head, nervously straightening her skirt. "I guess the biggest thing is that my husband and I aren't getting along very well. The smallest issue can turn into a fight between us. For instance, I stayed up late the other night folding clothes and ironing. He knew I had to get up as early as he did, that I had to feed the kids and get them off to school, but he didn't offer to help. He never offers to help. So I asked him to help this one time, and he blew up! That's how it is all the time with him. I do everything I can to make the marriage work, and he does nothing."

"The two of you are fighting a lot, then," I said.

"Yes," she sighed, "and if our relationship keeps going in the same direction, I'm afraid we will either stay miserable the rest of our lives or end up divorcing each other."

"You said that everything is going wrong. What else is bothering you?"

"I'm upset about my weight and how it affects my mood," she said. "The other morning I weighed myself, and I was ten pounds over what I should be. I mean, I really hate myself for putting on all the extra pounds I have. So while I was making breakfast, totally preoccupied with how fat I'd gotten, I ended up dropping my best glass pitcher full of orange juice all over the floor. Then what did I do but yell at the kids when they ran right through it and tracked it into the den. I actually made them get down on the floor and clean it up." She glanced down. "The only happy family member that morning was the dog," she added, glancing back up. "He loves orange juice."

I smiled uneasily, knowing full well that her story wasn't funny. "You sound pretty down on yourself for being overweight and also for how you let it affect you."

She nervously began picking lint from her skirt. "I hate myself over it, like I said. And I shouldn't have taken it out on the kids. I'm turning into an awful mother, too."

"What else is bothering you?"

"My work is okay, but I'm constantly worried I'm going to make a mistake which will get me in trouble. And the people I work with, they're all right, but I'm just not close to any of them. I feel like I'm going nowhere in all my relationships, not just at work but at church, too. I just can't make myself get close to anyone anymore. I've been rejected and disappointed so many times before. The bottom line is I don't have many close friends."

"You feel lonely but afraid to get close to others because you might get hurt. You mentioned church. Is it much help or comfort to you?" I asked.

She caught herself compulsively picking lint, folded her hands into her lap, and sighed: "Church isn't a great place, either. Everybody acts so happy, but it seems so superficial, you know? And besides, I always feel guilty because I know all the things I should be doing—things a good Christian should do—and I don't do any of them. I just know God's disgusted with me. I can almost feel it. I'm definitely disgusted with myself."

Janet was obviously miserable. If you had asked her what caused her misery, she'd probably have told you that her marriage, her weight problem, her poor mothering, being lonely, plus many other things were the problem.

Would you be surprised, though, if I said Janet was missing the *real* cause of her emotional problems?

The real cause was the *lies* she was telling herself. She believed a whole list of emotionally destructive lies, and those were the fundamental reason for her misery.

What are some of those lies? Unless you are trained to look for them, you may not have even noticed she was telling herself any lies at all. But she was. Let's look closely at four of the many lies she unknowingly revealed to me, and let's compare them to the truth. She was telling herself that:

  • making mistakes is awful, when the truth is that

people make mistakes all the time and they are rarely catastrophic. To be human is to make mistakes. This is the "I Must Be Perfect" lie we'll discuss in the "Self Lies" chapter.

• her husband was causing all the marriage problems, when the truth is that she was equally responsible for them. This is the "It's All Your Fault" lie we'll study in the "Marital Lies" chapter.

• being overweight made her a rotten person, when the truth is that being overweight had little, if anything, to do with her worth as a human being. This is the "You Are Only As Good As What You Do" lie we'll explore in the "Worldly Lies" chapter.

• God was disgusted with her because she wasn't doing "Christian" things, when the truth is that God loves her regardless of how she behaves. This is the "God's Love Must Be Earned" lie, which we'll explain in the "Religious Lies" chapter.

Lest you think that Janet was uniquely plagued by lies, she wasn't. She was really no different from you and me. Most of us, like Janet, have bought into a whole batch of lies, and we're paying just as high an emotional price as she is. The more lies we believe, the more unhappy and emotionally troubled we are.

MOST OF OUR UNHAPPINESS AND EMOTIONAL STRUGGLES ARE CAUSED BY THE LIES WE TELL OURSELVES. *That* is a critically important truth—and the major premise of this book. And until we identify our lies and replace them with the truth, emotional well-being is impossible.

YOUR MENTAL TAPE DECK

Your brain is much like a tape deck. It can both record and play back, and it has access to a personal library of thousands of tapes ready to play at a moment's notice. These are tapes which hold all the beliefs, attitudes, and expectations that you have "recorded" during your life.

Some of the tapes inside your brain are truthful, such as "You can't please everybody all the time" or "Life is rough." Some of these tapes are lies, such as "I'm only as good as what I do" or "Life should be fair" or "Things have to go my way for me to be happy."

Many of your lie tapes have been around a long time, some even since childhood. You've listened to these tapes for so long that they feel true even though they are really lies. The longer a tape has been played, the more rigidly you believe it to be true.

Many lie tapes play in your mind without your even knowing it. They play unconsciously when life presses the play button. Unconscious or not, these tapes dramatically affect your feelings and actions each day. Ignorance is not bliss when it comes to these tapes. Unless they are made conscious, you are at their mercy.

Your emotional life hangs in the balance. It directly reflects whether your mind is dominated by lies or truth. If your mind has more lies than truth playing through it, you'll tend to be more emotionally unhappy and troubled. If, on the other hand, your mind has more truth than lies taped and running, you'll feel more well-being than misery. And if your mind is an equal mixture of both lies and truth, you will experience more of an up-and-down emotional experience. Both lies and truth want to control your tape deck, and whichever gains that control dictates what your life will be like.

The primary challenge, then, is not to attempt changing the circumstances surrounding us, although there is nothing wrong with improving them when we can. The primary challenge is to make our mental tapes as truthful as we can so that we will be able to handle successfully whatever circumstances come our way.

Lies produce emotional misery.

Truth produces emotional health.

It's as simple as that. As James Allen put it in *As a Man Thinketh*, "Every thought seed sown or allowed to fall into the mind and to take root there produces its own. . . . Good thoughts bear good fruit, bad thoughts bad fruit."[1]

This "law" that governs the psychological world—that thoughts bear after their own kind—is actually one of the greatest messages of personal hope for us. Why? Because it makes emotional well-being available to anyone who is willing to dedicate him- or herself to knowing, believing, and practicing truth.

This book will help you develop the knowledge, the awareness, and the tools to do just that.

WHAT ARE LIES—AND WHAT IS TRUTH?

Before we go on any further, perhaps we need to define these two pivotal terms.

Simply put, lies are beliefs, attitudes, or expectations that don't fit reality. And we don't have to go out looking for them. They come to us. We learn our lies from a variety of sources—our parents, our friends, the culture we live in, even the church we attend—and they make life emotionally miserable, even unbearable.

Some of the lies we tell ourselves we know to be lies. But as I mentioned, some we believe have actually become the "truth" because we have practiced them for so long. These are the most dangerous lies of all because we rarely, if ever, dispute them. We don't dispute what we believe to be true.

What is the truth, then? Great question. A great answer, though, is hard to come by because truth can be such a difficult thing to uncover. Facts can be twisted, even innocently, to back whatever belief or lie we want them to. Remember, not too many centuries ago, the facts known at the time suggested that the world was flat. The Kennedy assassination is another excellent example. Even with all the available eyewitness, photographic, and physical evidence, experts still can't agree on how many assassins there were, how many shots were fired, where they were fired from, and who was behind it all. In the twenty-five years since JFK was shot, students of the "facts" are still not in agreement over the truth.

So what is truth? At the risk of making a classic understatement, truth is reality as it is, not as it seems to be. Can we know the unvarnished truth of a situation? Yes, but seeing and understanding the truth are skills that have to be learned, and as with most skills, learning them can be quite difficult and painful at times. But the more you practice, the better you get. The better you get, the healthier you become. The more you're able to see truth about yourself and life, the more you'll be able to see past your lies' smokescreens, and that is one of the skills this book can help you develop.

I want to add one important caveat about truth. I believe that certain truths, "ultimate truths" that give focus and meaning and substance to life, can only be learned through spiritual means. Truth is like an iceberg, really. What we can learn from our day-to-day experiences is just the tip of the truth that we can learn on our own. Knowing the deeper, spiritual truths of life that lie below life's surface requires that we depend on a greater power than ourselves. It seems planned that way. To learn the truths that are the most powerful and life-sustaining of all, we must look to that greater power.

JANET AND HER LIES—A CLOSER LOOK

Let's go back to Janet. She was totally unaware of the lies causing her unhappiness. Remember that she was much more focused on the external circumstances of her life, convinced that those circumstances have to change before she can be happy. Let me show you how, through simple questions and answers, with truth as the guide, I helped Janet to see her situation.

"Janet, you mentioned that you worry a lot about making mistakes. Do you always get down on yourself when you mess up?" I asked.

"Well, yes. I shouldn't make mistakes, especially the ones I've made before," she said.

"Why not?"

"What do you mean, why not?" she said, stiffening. "Because mistakes are stupid; because smart people don't make mistakes."

"Do you mean you don't think you're smart if you ever make a mistake?" I asked.

"Well, I don't *feel* too smart, that's for sure."

"So you don't feel too smart or like yourself when you yell at the kids or drop a glass or put on a pound or two?" I asked.

"Not too many people like fat, clumsy, angry mothers," she said, with a sarcastic smirk.

"They don't?"

She eyed me. "You know what I mean. . . ."

"No, I don't think I do. What do you mean?"

"Do you like *yourself* when *you* make mistakes?" she said, trying to turn the tables.

"I sure don't like that I made the mistake, but I try not to make it an issue of self-esteem," I calmly gazed at Janet. "Is that what you're doing?"

"Self-esteem!" She frowned in thought a moment. "Well, maybe. But . . . I have to shoot for the best. I *want* to do the best I can at everything!"

"Do you know anyone who does his best at everything?" I countered.

Looking caught, she replied, "No, not really."

"So you are trying to live up to a goal you've never seen anyone else achieve?" I asked.

"Well . . ."

"And if you fail to live up to it, what does that say about you? That you're no good?"

"Well . . . I have to admit that I feel no good, but yes, I know, in my head, it doesn't really mean I'm no good," she finally confessed.

"Janet, play psychologist for a minute. Do you see any lies you are telling yourself in all this?"

"Lies?"

"Yes, lies."

"No, not really," she answered.

"How does this one sound? 'I can't accept myself unless I'm perfect.'"

"Why is that a lie?"

"Because, simply, it doesn't fit reality. Nobody is perfect, and if you wait until you're perfect before you accept yourself, you'll wait the rest of your life."

She arched an eyebrow. "Okay, okay. You made your point."

"Let me ask you something," I said. "How do you think people would respond to you if you *were* perfect? Would they like you better? Before you answer, think about the people you know that seem 'perfect.'"

"Well, no, since you put it that way . . . 'Perfect' people are a bit hard to be around," she said, fidgeting again. "Dr. Thurman, what are you saying?"

I leaned over and said: "You are telling yourself lie after lie after lie and believing them all. That is why you're so depressed. But—you can get rid of them—and your depression—if you are willing to put the time and effort in." I paused. She was staring at me, somewhat surprised. "For instance, what one lie might you be telling yourself about your weight?"

"A lie? Well . . ." she mumbled, thinking.

"How did you feel fixing breakfast this morning?" I said.

"That's easy. I felt ugly. I felt stupid and worthless because I couldn't lose ten pounds."

"And what might the lie be if you are wrong about your feelings?"

"I suppose something like I've got to be slim to be worth something?" She paused, sat back on the couch, crossed her arms, and added, "Or that I have to live up to other people's standards. I guess those are lies, really. I guess I've always known that, even though it doesn't make me feel any different."

"Still, that's a good start," I told her, and it was. Janet would soon see many more of her lies and how they controlled her life, and she could then slowly and surely get rid of them.

Are you wondering what your own lies are? Take a minute to complete the following self-analysis questionnaire to find out. Read each statement and indicate your agreement/disagreement with it using the following scale:

1	2	3	4	5	6	7
strongly disagree			neutral			strongly agree

Do not spend too much time on any one statement, but give the answer which describes how you really feel. Try to avoid using the neutral (4) response.

_____ 1. I must be perfect.

_____ 2. I must have everyone's love and approval.

_____ 3. It is easier to avoid problems than to face them.

_____ 4. Things have to go my way for me to be happy.

_____ 5. My unhappiness is externally caused.

_____ 6. You can have it all.

_____ 7. You are only as good as what you do.

_____ 8. Life should be easy.

_____ 9. Life should be fair.

_____ 10. You shouldn't have to wait for what you want.

_____ 11. People are basically good.

_____ 12. My marriage problems are my spouse's fault.

_____ 13. If my marriage takes hard work, my spouse and I must not be right for each other.

_____ 14. My spouse should meet all of my needs.

_____ 15. My spouse owes me for what I have done for him/her.

_____ 16. I shouldn't have to change who I am in order to make my marriage better.

_____ 17. My spouse should be like me.

_____ 18. I often make mountains out of molehills.

_____ 19. I often take things personally.

_____ 20. Things are black and white to me.

_____ 21. I often miss the forest for the trees.

_____ 22. The past predicts the future.

_____ 23. I often reason things out with my feelings rather than the facts.

_____ 24. God's love can be earned.

_____ 25. God hates the sin and the sinner.

_____ 26. Because I'm a Christian, God will protect me from pain and suffering.

_____ 27. All of my problems are caused by my sins.

_____ 28. It is my Christian duty to meet all the needs of others.

_____ 29. Painful emotions such as anger, depression, and anxiety are signs that my faith in God is weak.

_____ 30. God can't use me unless I am spiritually strong.

Each of the statements listed above is a lie or a way that we lie to ourselves. Thus, the more you agreed with each statement, the more you were agreeing with a lie. Go back through your responses and put a check mark by any statement that you gave a (5), (6), or (7) to. Those are the lies that you tend to believe the most and are the ones you may want to pay the most attention to as you read this book.

Attempting to see through your lies to the truth is tough. Trying to do it by yourself is even tougher. Consider this book a way—a potentially life-changing way—to see your lies for what they are and get back to living a life based on truth. In the following pages, we are going to unmask the lies we tell ourselves, the lies that masquerade as the truth, the lies that are making us miserable in marriage, in faith, in daily living. And then we are going to learn what we can do to get rid of those lies. As we do, you'll notice that many of the lies overlap a bit. Almost everyone is coping with a set of lies that feed into other lies.

As you read, you'll often feel you are reading about yourself, but you'll see your coworkers, friends, family, even your minister in these chapters too. We have many lies in common with those we know and love. We also have another thing in common—the ability to change. The truth about change, though, is that you must *want* to. Like Janet, we make our lives miserable, but also like

Janet, we can take steps to do something about it. To be healthy and whole emotionally, living contentedly with reality as it is, not as it seems—that's our goal.

So set that inner tape recorder of yours on "pause," and read on.

PART TWO

THE LIES WE BELIEVE

2.

SELF LIES

Nothing is so easy as to deceive one's self; for what we wish we readily believe.

Demosthenes

 othing ever goes my way."

Susan had begun counseling with me over an industrial-sized case of anger and bitterness. "I never get a break," she complained. "Like driving over here today. I got stuck behind this gravel truck. Suddenly gravel was everywhere, hitting my windshield! It cracked it! So I swerved to miss the rest, and this guy in the other lane wouldn't let me over—honked at me loud enough to wake the dead!"

"Pretty rough day. Yet, you sound like you think it's better for other people."

"Looks to me like it is. Other people are happy. I just don't understand why I'm always getting dumped on. Why did I get the rotten husband? Why didn't I get that job I wanted? Why does my windshield get cracked? Life should be easier, that's all."

Most of us feel a little like Susan every day of our lives. She believes other people have it easy, and she's got it tough. She believes everything has to go her way before

35

she can be happy. And when she's upset, it's because something or somebody has caused it. It didn't take long for Susan to find herself drowning in self-pity, unable to function, all because she believed a pack of lies—a pack of self-lies.

The lies that we deceive ourselves with, as Demosthenes suggested in his statement above, are often a function of what we *wish* were true whether it is or not. In fact, when such lies are brought to our attention, we often deny that we believe them because they seem so unrealistic or absurd. Susan certainly would. Our actions and emotions, though, reveal that we do, and those lies greatly influence the way we look at ourselves, others, and the world around us. The lies we'll discuss in this chapter are those most destructive to people I counsel. Let's start with one that's rampant in our success-oriented world.

"I Must Be Perfect"

Jim, a highly successful executive of a communication systems company, came to see me several years ago. He told me how he'd spent most of his life struggling with extreme feelings of inferiority and how he'd tried to overcome those feelings by being a super-achiever. Nothing he accomplished, though, made him feel better about himself. In fact, he was chronically depressed and felt little joy and satisfaction in life at all.

"I think the bottom line is that I hate myself," he told me one day.

"Why do you think you hate yourself?" I asked.

"Well, I never do things as well as they should be done."

"Never?"

"Never!" Jim said, his arms folded, back as stiff as a yardstick. I could tell it was an answer he had practiced many times.

Jim was saying something extraordinary. Most of us feel good about *something* we do. His answer shed a burst of light on his perfectionism fixation. "Jim, you know you're talented. I find it surprising to hear you say you have never done anything well enough to satisfy yourself."

"Yeah, well, it's true.

"Maybe your standards are too high."

Jim exploded. "My standards aren't too high! If I didn't shoot for the highest possible goals, I wouldn't be who I am."

"And being who you are, how do you feel?"

He looked at me quietly, deflated. He knew the answer to that one.

"Is it possible that your standards have become more important to you than your own peace and contentment?" I asked.

Although it was a moot question, Jim hedged his answer: "Still, there has to be a way for me to keep my standards and also have peace of mind."

This exchange with Jim captures how most perfectionists think. They have unrealistically high standards they have never met and can't possibly meet, yet they hang on to these standards as if they are objects of worship. Even when they begin to feel depressed, even suicidal, they see the idea of changing their standards as blasphemous. In a very painful way, the standards become more important than their very selves.

Each of us feels inferior to one degree or another, just as Jim does. As psychologist Alfred Adler puts it,

"To be human is to feel inferior." Some of us cope with inferiority feelings by accepting our imperfections and trying to do the best we can to improve them. Unfortunately, others struggle with these feelings by overcorrecting and trying to be perfect. It's as if we say to ourselves, "If I can just be perfect, then I can finally put these feelings of inferiority to rest and accept myself." Any drive for perfection, though, is doomed from the start.

What exactly is perfectionism? Dr. David Burns, a psychiatrist known for his studies in mood disorders like depression, offers a very good definition:

> I do *not* mean the healthy pursuit of excellence by men and women who take genuine pleasure in striving to meet high standards. Without concern for quality, life would seem shallow and true accomplishment would be rare. . . . I am talking about . . . those whose standards are high beyond reach or reason, people who strain compulsively and unremittingly toward impossible goals and who measure their own worth entirely in terms of productivity and accomplishment. For these people, the drive to excel can only be self-defeating.[1]

Sound like you? If so, you know all too well the emotional price one pays for being perfectionistic. The need to be perfect creates a no-win scenario. Why? Because when you attain the high goals you set, you'll tell yourself, "That really wasn't anything. That's what I should have done. No big deal." If you fall short of the same goal, though, you no doubt think, *What is wrong with me? What a stupid idiot I am! Can't I do anything right?*

Life soon becomes a never-ending series of "tests" that create constant anxiety concerning how well (or poorly) you'll perform, and you'll rarely give yourself a minute to feel good about yourself when you do excel.

Almost all perfectionists know at some level that being perfect is impossible. Yet most of the ones I've counseled feel they'd be quitters to lower their expectations to a realistic, livable level even when they finally see what unrealistic expectations are doing to their emotional well-being.

In reality, more than their emotional well-being is at stake. Many perfectionists end up like the sharp young lawyer who began coming to me last year when he couldn't shake suicidal feelings. This clean-cut man with a bright future couldn't see the good things he'd done for focusing on his shortcomings. Rather than change the perfectionism lie he was living, he was on the brink of killing himself for it. That's how strong lies can be in our lives.

What do perfectionists fear? They fear that if they don't keep their standards sky-high, they won't accomplish anything. They will be branded failures, and failing is our society's unforgivable sin. It's the dark side of our American "can-do" psyche. Ironically, though, America was founded by failures: people who couldn't make it in Europe came to America; then people who couldn't make it in the cities settled the wilderness. The best of the American spirit knows that success is not fearing failure, but learning from it. The perfectionists will not allow themselves that luxury.

If I sound exceptionally outspoken on this lie, it's because I battle it constantly. I can be self-critical and self-condemning with the best of them. For example, as a high school athlete, I'd hurl tennis rackets, slamming them on the court when I didn't play "perfectly." I broke so many rackets because of my perfectionistic anger, I kept the local sporting goods store in business for years. In college, it only got worse. I'd get so angry when I didn't play perfectly during tournaments that I'd yell unprintable words at the top of my voice. I made a fool of myself on more occasions than I care to discuss. Why? Because I felt that I wasn't a good person unless I did things perfectly. My mind knew that goal was impossible. But my gut didn't always agree.

So what can be done to fight this lie? Jim started to understand the answer. My conversation with him ended like this:

"Look, if I don't strive to be the best, I'll be mediocre, like everyone else," Jim said, admitting his biggest fear.

"Did you say the best? What's the difference between *the* best and *your* best?" I asked.

"They *should* be one and the same," Jim said.

"And if they aren't?" I asked.

"I'm a failure," he said in a quiet voice.

This is where he was stuck. Jim told himself his best should always be *the* best. He couldn't accept the possibility that he could never keep up such a pace. Now he sat tapping his fingers on the chair's arm.

"So, do you want to be a robot?" I said.

He stopped his tapping. "What?"

"Only a robot, something inhuman, could be that perfect."

Jim laughed. It was the first time I'd seen him laugh in several weeks. "Funny you should put it that way; I often feel like a robot or that I'm trying to be like one."

"And how does that feel?"

"Rotten!" Jim sighed. "It feels awful. I feel stuck. Clogged up. Like I can't be a normal person."

"That's it," I said. "Your perfectionism isn't really allowing you to be a normal human being. Jim, as paradoxical as it seems, I think you will find that developing more realistic standards will help you perform at the same high level you do now, if not higher."

Jim thought a minute. Then he said, "Okay, that sounds good in theory, but how do I know when I'm being realistic and not idealistic?"

"Why not look at your current performance level and let that be the baseline?" I suggested. "In other words, take your average performance in a given area and set a little higher goal instead of significantly higher. You're a golfer, right? What's your average golf score?"

"My handicap's sixteen," he said.

"That's the average number of strokes over par that you shoot, right?"

"Right."

"Wouldn't it be realistic to try to shave a stroke or two off your average rather than trying to shave off ten? I think you're trying to shave ten to fifteen strokes off your performance in life, and that's downright defeating."

Jim tapped his fingers on the chair's arm for a long moment, until finally he said, "Maybe. I'm beginning to see what you're getting at. I suppose we could work on specific goals, a little at time."

Perfectionism is a hard lie to break. Breaking it demands that the perfectionist treat him or herself with respect, allowing for the same mistakes as other mortals make and acknowledging that the efforts are worthy in and of themselves. Jim, like so many, is a casualty of the American "winner" mentality. Our sports, where winners are few and losers are filmed crying in the locker room, teach the devastating lesson that the virtue is not in the struggle but in the prize. Whether it be a Miss America runner-up or a guy who didn't get a promotion, second-best is not good enough. Perfection, being number one, is all.

With this kind of mindset, we produce millions upon millions of people who feel like losers because they were never "number one." The message to all of us seems to be: "It doesn't matter if you do the best you can; what matters is whether or not you win or lose." What a horribly destructive message to teach anyone! (Remember, winners often lose many times before they begin winning.) Thankfully, philosophers like Lord Houghton have advocated the truth that combats this lie: "The virtue lies in the struggle not the prize."

Jim is now someone breaking this self-destructive cycle. Oh, he's still a superachiever by nature and probably always will be, but he's slowly learning to enjoy his *efforts* as he holds himself up to his own personal standard instead of the world's.

"I Must Have Everyone's Love and Approval"

"Unless everybody loves and accepts me, I can't feel good about myself."

That's essentially what those who believe this lie are saying to themselves. Such people become social chameleons in that they often change their "color" to fit their interpersonal "terrain" so that they can keep everyone happy and gain everyone's approval. But after a few years of this, the chameleon loses all sense of self, his true "color" as a person. "Who am I? What am I really like? What do I really feel?" Those are the questions I hear from patients burdened by this lie.

Cindy grew up being a "pleaser," and she derived a lot of her worth from keeping people happy with her. Her grades were always good. She never caused her parents any problems, and she went along with her friends on most things. Now at twenty-three, she has begun to feel all the years of pleasing others might have some draw-backs. One of her first statements to me told the whole story: "I can't stand it when someone is upset with me. I feel like I have to do something to make them feel better toward me." Then she glanced down. She was not one for a lot of eye contact.

"Something happen recently?" I ventured.

"I started going to a church that's a different de-nomination from my parents' church. They don't like it and are putting pressure on me to switch back," she mumbled.

"How would you feel if you did?"

Cindy looked me straight in the eye. "I'd hate it. This new church really meets my needs, and I feel closer to God there. But Mom and Dad, they're making me crazy. I feel like I'm about to explode! I don't know what to do!"

"I get the impression you know what you want to do," I slowly said.

"I do? What? You mean, I want to go to this new church?"

"Isn't that what you're telling me? Don't let me put words in your mouth," I said, knowing full well she might try to please me too.

"Yes," she said quietly, "it is. I really want to stay there."

"What about your parents' approval?" I asked.

"Well, I hate not having it," she said. "Maybe I can explain it to them?"

"And if they don't understand?"

"I would feel horrible," she said. "I know I need to be more independent of what they think, but I really struggle with it."

Cindy's need for approval was a no-win scenario in the same way that perfectionism is. Even if you gain someone's approval today, you may not have it tomorrow.

Each day presents the same challenge: Can I gain and keep people's approval?

This lie puts your emotional well-being into the hands of people who may not be trustworthy. It gives a sizable amount of power over you to others, and some of those people, friends and family alike, may take advantage of it. Manipulation, especially from those nearest to you, is made way too easy. The victims, the pleasers, end up taking better care of others than of themselves, hiding their growing anger in the process.

Doug, a friend of mine, is approaching forty and could be described as a happy family man, the kind with two kids, a nice wife, and a cocker spaniel. Doug also has a strong need to please his mother, who lives three hundred miles away. Every Christmas, Thanksgiving, Easter, and Mother's Day since Doug left home, he spent with his mother, even after his marriage. Since his wife's family lived in the same city as his own, he felt that to be fair they should spend holidays with his mother. And when they would occasionally spend part of a holiday with her parents, they'd still make the long trek to his mother's for the rest of the holiday.

One Easter, Doug had been very busy at work and decided that he really wanted to stay home and spend a quiet holiday with his own family. His mother wasn't happy. She let Doug know in no uncertain terms that he wasn't being a very good son if he didn't come see her.

"I love my mother, Chris," he confided. "I do. But sometimes I think I'm neglecting my own family trying to please her."

Most of us can identify with this sort of bind. We think, "Should I do what I feel is right, knowing that others will not like it? Or should I keep others happy with me by doing what they want and ignoring my own convictions?"

The emotional fallout of this conflict is that we

bounce back and forth between guilt (over doing what we want at the expense of what others would have us do) and anger (over doing what others want at the expense of what we want to do). Anger or guilt. Not such a great choice, is it?

The truth is that some people aren't going to like us or what we do, no matter how hard we try. In the attempt to gain everyone's love and approval through chronic acquiescence, though, we may lose ourselves. How then to solve this dilemma? A good way is to keep telling yourself the truth (that you can't have everyone's approval and that trying to only makes your life worse) that will confound this lie every time you're caught in it. That way, as your subconscious is playing your lie tape, you will be hearing the truth consciously, and you may be able to control your emotions and make a reasoned decision. Psychologists call this process "self-talk," and we'll discuss the concept in detail later.

"It Is Easier to Avoid Problems Than to Face Them"

When I was a college professor, I noticed a very interesting phenomenon among my students. When I'd assign a reading assignment, some of the students would put off the assignment until the night before it was due. These were students who believed, at some conscious or unconscious level, that the best way to handle difficult situations in life was to avoid them. Oh, these "avoiders" wasted a lot of time worrying about the difficult assignment, but they still chose procrastination as the best alternative.

Other students took the approach of chipping away

at the assignment a little each day, which made a difficult assignment manageable and profitable.

These two groups were acting out both sides of the It Is Easier to Avoid Problems lie. The first group, "the avoiders," were the ones lying to themselves. The second group, "the facers," were the truthful ones. You can guess which group did better on the assignments.

In life the avoiders ignore problems until they either go away or get worse and have to be faced: that noise under the hood, the small extra charges on the credit card each month, the small conflict in their marriage. Prosperous, successful people don't bother with such frustrations, the avoiders tell themselves, and they avoid problems at all costs. Problems are for others, for losers. Of course, we all know that life has a way of becoming more painful if these problems are avoided while they pile up day after day. They just don't go away. They must be handled.

I am most concerned that too many parents today are unnecessarily rescuing their children from problems in misguided love powered by this lie. When parents make a habit of rescuing their child, the child begins believing this lie too—and it soon becomes a deeply ingrained "truth." These children, though, haven't been done a favor. They've been deprived of chances to develop the appropriate coping skills they'll need when life in all its unavoidable pain hits them head-on in adulthood. I firmly believe, barring certain severe situations beyond the child's ability to cope, that children need to be responsible for facing their own problems.

I struggle with this mixed-up love impulse with my son, Matthew, and my daughter, Ashley. My first wish is that both of them would go through life without a care, without ever having a need to cry or frown. On second thought, I realize the impossibility of that wish.

Recently, we began attending a new church. Matthew wasn't thrilled with the new Sunday school. And at a very high decibel level, he expressed his feelings each time we led him toward his classroom. It's an awful feeling to walk away from your crying, frightened child. For six Sundays in a row, I wanted to say to heck with it, turn around, grab him up, and take him into "big" church with us. That short-term action would have been satisfying. The long-term result, though, would have been destructive. He'd begin to expect my help, and I'd be stuck in a pattern of rescue. So I stuck it out, confronted my pain, and made Matthew confront his. And soon he grew to enjoy his teachers and classmates.

When we believe that our problems will go away if we avoid them, we ask for emotional problems. As psychiatrist Scott Peck noted in *The Road Less Traveled:*

> Fearing the pain involved, almost all of us, to a greater or lesser degree, attempt to avoid problems. We procrastinate, hoping that they will go away. We ignore them, forget them, pretend they do not exist. . . . We attempt to get out of them rather than suffer through them.
>
> This tendency to avoid problems and the emotional suffering inherent in them is the primary basis of all human mental illness.[2]

Those who avoid their pain usually end up with more pain in the long run. Those who face their pain save themselves a great deal of unnecessary suffering. It's as simple as that.

"I Can't Be Happy Unless Things Go My Way"

I once had a teenage client who was quite obsessive about things having to go a certain way for him to have a "good day," so I asked him to write a list of what would have to happen for a day to be a good one. His incredibly detailed list began like this:

- Waking up to a favorite song playing on the clock radio
- Wearing a specific set of clothes and tennis shoes
- Not having to eat oatmeal, scrambled eggs, or bran cereal.
- Getting the front seat on the school bus
- All his friends saying nice things to him all day long.

The list went on so long and was so detailed that it was literally impossible for all the things to go just as he wanted. Consequently, he'd never had a happy day. Something always spoiled it.

Be honest: Are you the type who can't enjoy a movie if someone sits in front of you? Can you enjoy a meal if the service is slow? And I bet you've never gotten mad when you get stuck behind a poky driver on a crowded highway, right?

In reality, traffic lights don't change when you want them to, people talk when you wish they wouldn't, spouses are unkind when you want kindness, and lines are long when you're in a hurry. Those who can't be happy unless things always go their way are headed for ulcers, migraines, and a lot of personal unhappiness.

The other day I stuck a videotape in our VCR and the tape popped straight back out. Since our VCR doesn't have an "automatic eject" feature, I flipped open the cover and guess what—inside our expensive VCR were two toy cars, a toothbrush, and a couple of Band-Aids!! My young son had stored his prized possessions inside the little plastic door. At that moment, with an expensive repair bill dancing through my brain, I was more than a little angry that life wasn't going my way. And, at that same moment, I could either tell myself the lie that I couldn't be happy if it didn't or the truth that life could go however it liked, and I could still be content.

Those of us who suffer from the My Way lie tend to believe the world revolves around us to one degree or another. This narcissistic style of living makes us personally miserable; worse though, it makes placing ourselves in another person's shoes all but impossible, and that incapacity makes healthy and stable relationships all but impossible.

I see the My Way lie at its worst in marriage counseling. The "I" in many marriages is so strong that the "We" is never allowed to develop. These marriages then, become nothing more than two "My Way's" pulling in separate directions.

Jon and Debbie, an attractive young couple I've been counseling, come to mind. They had been college sweethearts, inseparable. But during each session they had with me, they sat at opposite ends of my couch. For five years they'd been married, and, except for the first few months, their whole marriage had been a battle of wills.

"I feel Debbie never understands how I feel," Jon began in one session.

"I feel the same way about you," Debbie chimed in. "You're always so locked into what you want that what I want never gets noticed."

"That isn't true. I do things for you all the time," Jon answered.

"Only things you don't mind doing," Debbie muttered, inching even farther into the corner of the couch.

"Okay," I said, "Let's stop a minute. How do both of you feel about the word *we*?"

They both looked at me as if I'd lost my mind.

"What?" Debbie finally said.

"The *I* in your marriage is stronger than the *we*, and it's causing both of you to be resentful. Do you think in *I* or *we* terms?"

"Well, I guess mostly *I*," Jon said, leaning closer, his eyebrows cocked in the suspicious position.

"It's obvious that both of you are suffering a great deal," I said. "Even when one of you gets your way, you do it at the expense of the other person, which, again, makes both of you suffer."

"Well," Jon paused, glancing at Debbie, "I do get so intent on fighting Debbie on specific issues that I don't realize we both end up worse off."

Then Jon explained how the night before they had wanted to go see a movie. Of course, it wasn't the same movie, and neither wanted to sacrifice and see the other's choice. Whose movie, he asked, should they go see? The stubborn childishness of the question may look silly in print, but we all know mature couples who fight over these things every day. The My Way lie becomes a Custer's Last Stand—a "My Way or No Way" attempt for control. The *we* sense of sacrifice is not important.

While we were talking about simple negotiating, though, Debbie said something quite revealing. "What is silly," she said, "is I used to like doing things for Jon before everything got to be a big fight."

"Thinking *we* doesn't mean acting like your feelings don't matter," I explained. "You're just working hard not to let them matter so much that the *we* is unnecessarily damaged, that you don't want to do anything for each other anymore."

"But what if going along with him compromises my values?" Debbie said. "See, Jon is willing to go to R-rated movies, and I'm not."

"That's a good point. Sometimes personal values and ethics need to be stood up for at the expense of marital harmony. But, in general, the *we* needs to be more important than the *I* when it comes to marriage. With a little practice, the difference will become obvious." And that's what I suggested to them.

Then, before my eyes, I watched Jon move a little toward Debbie on the couch, and say, "Well, I guess we could try to differentiate between the two." And even more surprisingly, Debbie smiled.

The same can be said for everyone, married or not. With practice we can sit through a movie with someone in front of us. We can enjoy the day even though we aren't wearing the right outfit. We can see that the world is not exactly our oyster, that we can't make every irritation a pearl, but that we can be content anyway.

Life has a nasty habit of reminding us it will not be totally controlled, and if we don't believe it, we can watch for the next proof. When it comes, we have two options: petulantly, we can burst a blood vessel, demanding life to go our way, which of course it often won't; or we can learn to be flexible, to cope with what life throws us, and to be content in spite of who's getting whose way.

"It's Somebody Else's Fault"

"You make me furious when you do that!"

One of the underlying themes of this book is that our way of thinking about the events of our lives is what makes or breaks us emotionally. The last lie said that I must have my own way before I can be happy. This lie takes that idea one unhealthy step further. It allows me to pass the buck for all my emotional upsets onto anybody and anything nearby. It points a finger outward. No responsibility is taken here.

You are the one making *me* furious.

Picture yourself in a very, very long line. It is not moving. You are getting angrier by the minute, stamping your foot, looking at your watch. The woman in front of you, though, is cool, calm, and dry as if she's enjoying the respite from hurrying 'and scurrying. Now consider this: Is it really the long line that upsets you or just the way you choose to think about it? If it is the event that is upsetting you, then why isn't the woman ahead of you feeling exactly the way you are?

You might say, "Okay, but what about certain events that do lead to the same emotional reaction in most people, like the death of a loved one?" The event is still not causing the emotional reaction. The people involved share the same belief system, the belief that death is a bad thing, and that is why they are all reacting in a similar way.

But even in this case, we can all think of examples when the death of a loved one brought a variety of feelings. For instance, Grandpa, a devout man of faith, has been suffering painfully for months with a terminal illness. The Christians in the family might react to his death with relief and calm, believing his suffering is over and he is now with God, while the nonreligious family members might react with the same relief but none of the comfort. It is still the same event, but each person filters his or her reactions through his or her specific internal view of the event.

Of course, the Somebody Else's Fault lie pervades every aspect of life, every relationship, every action. Thirty-year-old Beth based much of her life on it without a hint of what was happening to her. One day, she told me of her sister who would call and literally waste hours of her time "droning on about her problems." Beth blamed these calls and many other things for her constant misery. When she finished the story, I suggested she tell her sister how she felt. Beth looked surprised. "I couldn't do that. It would hurt her feelings," she said. As many patients do, Beth was stiff-arming some advice that might really help her.

"What if I said your sister isn't the problem. That you are," I said—and waited.

She looked even more surprised. "*I'm* not causing my problems. She is, by being so insensitive!" she almost barked at me.

"So it's her fault that you are mad at her?" I asked.

"Exactly," she answered, sitting back in her chair. "How could I possibly be the problem when it's her calling me that makes me angry?"

"Are you the only one she calls?"

"Good grief, no!" she said.

"Any of the others get as angry as you do?"

Beth frowned. "I don't know. I guess it's possible they don't. I'm not sure where you're heading," she said, turning a little away from me.

"Well, let's say you call ten people for donations to a charity," I said. "Four of them hang up on you, three politely tell you they don't want to contribute, and three gladly give. All ten of them got the same phone call from you, but you got three different kinds of reactions. Are you to blame for the different reactions?"

"No," she said. "I don't guess I could be, could I? The way they reacted had more to do with the way they are." She stopped and looked at me out of the corner of her eye. "I get what you're saying. It's my problem, not hers—is that it?"

In realizing that truth, Beth was giving herself the chance to move from the victim role of "Look what she does to me!" to the healthier role of seeing what she was doing to herself and taking action by telling her sister how she felt.

"*Men are disturbed not by things but by the view they take of them,*" said the ancient philosopher Epictetus. Unfortunately, when we view life through glasses fogged by lies, we don't see life as clearly as we need to. The point of Epictetus's great truth is that what happens to us isn't nearly as important as how we choose to think about it, as we saw in Beth's case.

Assume you are in a store and need some assistance. You ask the salesperson to help you.

"Look, you imbecile, can't you see this isn't my department?" the clerk responds.

Let's assume you become quite angry about this response and answer, "Don't call me an imbecile, you jerk. How dare you treat me this way. I'll have your job!"

What caused your reaction? Most people would answer it was the rudeness of the salesperson, no doubt about it. Epictetus would point out that the clerk's treatment of you was just a triggering event that cannot by itself make you angry. Your view of the clerk's behavior is what causes you to get angry. It's really your choice.

Okay, this may sound like psychobabble, but think about the implications of Epictetus' truth: we can't blame *events* for our feelings because our *feelings* are caused by our *thoughts*.

How *could* you have responded to that clerk? Look at it this way: Does he know from personal experience that you are imbecilic, and has he just stated the truth? Or is *his* anger *his* problem? Obviously, he has allowed his own externals to make him angry, and he's taking it out on you, the innocent bystander. At that moment, you choose whether you allow his problem to become yours.

The bottom line is that we mold our emotional lives by the way we choose to think about what happens to us. To think otherwise is to be emotionally irresponsible, to place responsibility for our well-being in the hands of every little event life throws at us. How we respond is, after all, our choice alone.

HOW TO DEFEAT YOUR LIES

Now you've gotten a taste of some of the lies we tell ourselves and the amazing hold they have over us emotionally—plus you've gotten a sample of the ways to defeat those lies.

Here, and at the end of each of the next four chapters, we'll discuss at length a "How-To," for combating your lies—and believe me, it is combat. You are fighting to get your life back, freeing it from all the lies that hold it hostage.

Before you can do anything about your lies, though, you first must know which lies you believe, right? You have to identify them and then understand them as much as possible. That's where I want us to start.

One of the best approaches for identifying lies in our lives was developed by psychologist Albert Ellis. It's called the ABC approach, and it's deceivingly simple. It requires a pencil and a pad to be your journal and some on-the-spot self-awareness:

- *A* represents the event that happens to you, that triggers a lie. It can be a major incident or a minor one, anything from being late for an appointment to being fired from a job.
- *B* represents "self-talk," what you mentally tell yourself about the event. Your self-talk can be a lie or a truth or a mixture of both.
- *C* represents your emotional reaction to that "self-talk." It can be anything from joy to despair.

Let's try it.

A—*THE EVENT:* Picture yourself in the ten-item express line at the grocery store. A woman in front of you is taking her sweet time, chatting with the checker, scolding her kids, picking up last minute items from the nearby racks, and then taking forever to write her check. You also notice she has more than ten items! In your journal, you will write down this event just as it happened.

B—*THE SELF-TALK:* Ordinarily you will notice your emotional reaction next (What do you feel? Frustrated? Irritated? Angry?). That's "C" of the ABC approach. That's not the true order, as you can see. Events cannot cause emotions (A cannot jump to C). They can only trigger our self-talk (B). Identifying your self-talk, then, is the hardest part of this approach, but it's also the key to it.

So there you stand in the line stifling your frustration, irritation, and anger so that you can analyze the self-talk that's causing your emotions. As you gaze at the woman slowly fumbling with her checkbook, you might think, "Okay. What am I saying to myself here?" Then you begin your analysis. "Let's see," you say. "I am telling myself:

"Things have to go my own way for me to be happy. That is, this line has to speed up for me to be happy."

"I/Everybody else should be perfect. That is, this woman should have had her act together before she got in this line. She's imperfect and that's inexcusable."

"My unhappiness is externally caused. That is, this person's taking so long is making me angry."

Do you get it? When you write this self-talk down in your journal, keep in mind that your self-talk in almost every encounter will be one of the lies we discuss in this book, or a variation of it. As you try this approach throughout your day, always work to pick out the general lie first, then your own variation of it. When keeping your ABC journal, always be as specific as you can about the exact lie you're telling yourself.

C—*THE EMOTIONAL REACTION:* What is your immediate emotional reaction? Is it frustration, irritation, then anger? Whatever it is, write it down in your journal. Why, you may even growl a bit at the checker when she finally gets to you, right?

Afterward, once you've gotten through the line, grabbed your bag of groceries, and headed for your car, take a moment to write this whole event, from A to C into your ABC journal, or keep it vividly in your mind until you can write it down. Analyze your self-talk a bit. How did you feel in that line as you became aware of what was causing your emotions? Did you feel better? Write that down. You may have remained frustrated, irritated, and increasingly angry in the line, even though you became aware of your self-talk. If your emotions didn't change, write that down. If you became not only frustrated, irritated, and angry at the woman but also yourself, write that down. If you stay upset for another thirty minutes, write that down too.

I usually have my patients keep an ABC journal for at least a couple of weeks before moving on to other assignments. Try it. I think you'll be surprised at the insight you will gain into your own style of dealing with life. You will begin to see some of the same lies pop out. You may begin, for instance, to see that you are telling yourself the I Must Have Everyone's Approval lie or the I/Everybody Must Be Perfect lie over and over. That knowledge is something you can work with. Don't be surprised if your self-analysis *doesn't* instantly change your attitude. That will come later.

Most importantly, though, keeping the ABC journal *will* make you see more clearly the lies that make your life unnecessarily troubled. We'll be adding this newfound skill of yours to the How-To's that follow.

Next, let's look at the large group of lies we learn from the world we live in and the truth we need to know about them.

3.

WORLDLY LIES

The truth must essentially be regarded as in
conflict with this world; the world has never
been so good, and will never become so good
that the majority will desire the truth.

Soren Kierkegaard

GRAB FOR ALL THE GUSTO!
LOOK OUT FOR NUMBER ONE!
DO YOUR OWN THING!

Advertisements, television shows, movies, maga-
zines, even books, are shouting such messages at
us every day in every way. And in childlike acceptance, we listen and believe. We look for truth in a jingle.
 Part of our willingness to believe may be wishful
thinking. Wouldn't it be nice if these messages were true?
Part of it may be the child within us who wants to believe
that someone wouldn't tell us something if it weren't
true. Whatever the reason, many of us rarely test the va-
lidity of the messages swirling around us.

How trustworthy, though, are these messages? Many,
if not most, are nothing less than dangerous. Yet we are
so inundated with these lies, minute by minute, day to
day, that they appear not only harmless but true.

Of course, most are not true—and the more we listen and believe, the more needless emotional misery we

create for ourselves. Let's take a look at the most wide-spread and dangerous of these worldly lies.

"You Can Have It All"

Who says you can't have it all? A popular beer commercial asks that question. It sounds like a child daring someone to tell him the awful truth: "Who *says* I can't have it all?"

Life says you can't, that's who. As the cliché goes, "You can't have your cake and eat it, too." Now *that* is a truth to live by.

Even though you've heard that cliché over and over again—be honest—Do you still think you can have it all?

If you're like most people today, you're nodding yes. We think we can, and not only that, we think we *should* have it all. Why? Because we look around and see others whose lives seem free from the struggle and pain in ours. They are financially secure, intelligent, attractive, or all three, and we believe that with just the right breaks we can have it all just as they obviously do.

Jim is one of "them." He is a highly successful business contractor, and, from every indication, he lives the American Dream. He drives a Mercedes, wears a Rolex watch, is a member of not one but three country clubs. His wife is attractive and intelligent, they have three great kids, and they all go on exotic vacations whenever they like. Beyond all that, he is well known and liked, so his life begins to take on storybook proportions. Jim is worth millions of dollars. In fact, though, Jim is one of the most unhappy patients I've ever had.

"I always thought when I reached this level of life I'd be happy," he said the first day he visited my office. He slouched low in the chair in front of me. "I know this sounds crazy, but all the things I have don't make me happy. They've actually become a burden."

"A burden?" I asked. "How?"

"We have more debts than ever. All that we own is just that much more to take care of. And, I don't know, it just seems the more we get, the more we want, you know?" he said, fiddling with his diamond pinky ring.

"Like what?"

"Right now we live in an expensive home, but we've got our eye on an even more expensive one. It's in a nicer neighborhood and all. My wife really wants to move. But the mortgage, I have to admit, will really put a lot of pressure on me."

"And that pressure is something you wouldn't like?"

"Well, normally, my work is always under some pressure, but this would be more than ever." He ran his hand through his head of distinguished grey hair. "If we don't move, though, my wife will be very upset."

"She's pushing you?" I asked.

"Yes . . . but I want to move over there, too."

"So keeping up with the Joneses isn't making you very happy," I added.

"I'm embarrassed to admit it, but it's true," he said, glancing down at the floor, then back up at me. "Sounds greedy, doesn't it? I mean, having it all never stops. We never say no to ourselves, but things don't seem to change much. Except I'm more miserable."

Do you want to know the truth? The truth is I have *never* met a person who really had it all. Never! Think of that someone who you think has it all. Odds are—very good odds—that if you scratched the surface of that someone's life, you'd find a life with painful gaps.

The best case study for this lie is found in the Bible— the great King Solomon. According to the biblical record, our man Solomon was the John D. Rockefeller,

Albert Einstein, and Hugh Hefner of his day all rolled into one very special person. He was the wealthiest and the wisest man on the earth during his life, and he denied himself no pleasure.

> I made my works great, I built myself houses, and planted myself vineyards. . . . I made myself water-pools. . . . I had greater possessions of herds and flocks than all who were in Jerusalem before me. I also gathered for myself silver and gold and the special treasures of kings and of the provinces. I acquired male and female singers, the delights of the sons of men, and musical instruments of all kinds. So I became great and excelled more than all who were before me in Jerusalem. Also my wisdom remained with me. Whatever my eyes desired I did not keep from them.[1]

Now, I don't know about you, but I'd consider that having it all. You'd think Solomon would have been quite content. Yet listen to some of his conclusions:
• "The abundance of the rich will not permit him to sleep."[2]
• "He who loves silver will not be satisfied with silver."[3]
• "I have seen all the works that are done under the sun; and indeed, all is vanity and grasping for the wind."[4]

In Solomon's efforts to have it all, he had everything but the one thing that completes it—happiness. The end result of the You Can Have It All lie is dissatisfaction with what one has and a vain "grasping for the wind." Many of us live our lives around the adage "The grass is always greener on the other side of the fence," and we work hard to get on that side. Those who do make it over, though, often find that their expectations were higher than reality.

The simple point is this: There isn't a side of the fence where we finally have it all and where the incessant craving for greener grass ceases. If we truly believe we can and should have it all, we never will. The attitude itself makes whatever we get less than enough. The more we expect, the more it takes to satisfy us.

Paul had the right attitude in his wise words to Timothy: "For we brought nothing into this world, and it is certain we can carry nothing out. And having food and clothing, with these we shall be content."[5] Isaac Bickerstaffe, a man from another century, put it this way: "If I am content with little, enough is as good as a feast." That's a great truth.

My wife, Holly, and I are not different from most other couples. We lived in an apartment when I was a college professor, and we dreamed of the day we'd own our own home. We were both sure that if we ever had our own home, we would be content, no matter how large or small that home might be. Well, now we own our home, and at first, we were quite content. Then we began noticing how much nicer and bigger other couples' houses were. We began noticing the bigger and better neighborhoods around our area and have even admitted to each other we wouldn't mind moving "up" a step. But now I wonder, if we actually moved to one of those nicer homes, would we not begin all too soon wanting something even nicer, just like Jim? Probably. I think the need for more is that insatiable.

Too many of my patients are materially and physically blessed yet are bitter because they don't have more. It's the way we are. I wish I could say we are a country content with little, but the fact is we are a country that demands and *expects* a feast. Keeping up with the Joneses is not so much an attitude as a destiny.

The Have It All lie, though, is an impossible, unhealthy dream that cheapens the rest of life, making us live for the future instead of enjoying the present. Very few of us are immune to it, but all of us have the choice whether to live by it.

"You Are Only As Good As What You Do"

"I haven't closed a deal in months," said Ted, who is a real estate developer. Things were rolling along fine in his life until the real estate market in his area went belly up. Because he was depressed and couldn't shake it, he came to see me.

"We keep dipping into savings to get by. That can't last forever," he moaned. He sat, hunched over his knees, his hands massaging his temples.

"How does doing that feel?"

He stopped, sitting straight up. "I hate it. I've never been so depressed. I'm normally an 'up' kind of guy! This has never happened to me before," he exclaimed.

"Before the real estate market went bad, how did you feel?" I asked.

He sat back in his chair. "Oh, I felt great."

"Are you saying your self-esteem has gone up and down with the market?" I asked him pointblank.

"Well . . . I guess you could put it that way."

"Okay, let's follow that thought. You feel good about yourself when things are going well. So does that mean you're only as worthwhile as your performance?"

"Now, I don't like looking at it *that* way . . ." he paused.

"Is it true?"

"Yeah, maybe," he mumbled. "I mean, I know I like myself a lot better when things are going good."

Our culture has an obsession with performance. We want to know how many "widgets" a salesman sold, how many hits a baseball player gets, how many A's a student made, how much money a worker made, how many degrees an applicant has, and on and on. These are somehow the signs of being a "success." Somehow we've gotten character and integrity mixed up with externals—if the salesman, for instance, sells a million widgets, he must be a great man. While this attitude may be an inescapable part of our competitive living, it has created a feeling in many of us that we are only as good as our last "performance."

You may remember the story of Kathy Ormsby. It was 1986 in Indianapolis, Indiana, the site of the NCAA track and field championships. Kathy was a pre-med honor student and track star at North Carolina State University. She also happened to be the collegiate record holder in the women's ten-thousand meter run. Something quite startling happened during the championship race. Kathy fell behind and couldn't seem to catch the front-runner. In a startling move, she ran off the track and out of the stadium to a nearby bridge, where she jumped off. The forty-foot fall permanently paralyzed her from the waist down.

Not knowing Kathy personally, I can only guess that her own perfectionism and tendency to equate her worth with performance created internal pressure she couldn't handle—all that talent and ability felled by lies.

Many of these driven people reach the point of suicide when their tendency to equate worth with performance makes them experience feelings of failure and self-hate.

Of course, like most lies, this one has a grain of truth in it. Our performances in life do say *something* about us. They are never complete representations of who we are, though. The *A* or *F* a student makes on a report card is never a statement that they are *A* or *F* persons, yet that is exactly how grades are misinterpreted by students, their parents, and often their teachers. A person's income level is never a statement about his or her value as a human being, yet in our society, the message is all too often, "You are only a worthwhile person if you rise up the corporate ladder, live in a big home in the suburbs, drive an expensive car, have a gold-colored charge card, wear the designer labels. . . ." You could finish the list for me. But nothing, nothing could be further from the truth.

It's a tough lie to crack. Our How-To at the end of the chapter will help. For now, though, let's look at Ted's train of thought during the rest of his session.

"That sounds a little silly, now, I know," said Ted, shrugging, "the fact that I like myself better when I'm doing well at work. But I put so much of myself into it. And when I was on top, I had everybody else telling me what a winner I was. It's just natural to like yourself more like that."

"Maybe in that light the real estate market's going bad is a good thing for you," I suggested.

"Whoa," he said, raising his hands. "Back up. How could it be good for me?"

"Well, it may give you a chance to see that you are basing your self-acceptance on how you do and what you do—not who you are."

"Yeah, well, who am I without what I do?" he asked in a low voice out of the side of his mouth.

"Well, you could base your self-esteem on something more stable," I suggested.

"Like what?" he asked.

"*You've* got to answer that," I said, and I waited.

Ted stared at me a moment, shuffled his feet, then said, "I guess that's where we need to keep talking."

What then should be the basis of self-esteem? I believe that comes from who made us, not what we do. We need to view ourselves in "vertical" dimensions—seeing who we are in God's eyes, not the "horizontal" dimensions of doing all we can to impress others through achievement or success. How does God the Creator see us? "A little lower than the angels" and "crowned . . . with glory and honor."[6] We are "fearfully and wonderfully made" and valuable enough to be purchased with the blood of his son.[7]

God sees us having great worth because he created us in his image. Now that is a true basis for self-esteem. Living this truth, though, is harder than believing it. How can we find healthy self-esteem in a world that caters to what we do instead of who we are? Others have gone the route of Solomon, striving for achievement, power, success, material possessions, sexual prowess, in an effort to feel good about themselves. What they find, though, is usually the same feeling of futility that Solomon did. Dodging this lie and the exhausting effort that it commands is all that keeps us from going down the same sad road.

Who are you without what you do? Essentially, we all have to ask ourselves the same question if we're ever going to find a solid basis for understanding our own innate worth. Then we have to work at giving ourselves a solid answer.

"Life Should Be Easy"

Automatic dishwashers, power steering, garage door openers, central air conditioning. Let's face it. Of all the people on earth, we Americans have the most gadgets designed to make our lives easier. The moment we have them, we all but decide we can't live without them.

Now, granted, there seems to be nothing wrong with making life as difficulty-free as possible. Inventing ways to make our existence easier makes good sense. What causes trouble is that this attitude often flips into one that *demands* life, in all its complex glory, to be easy.

When we think this way, we give ourselves over to the pleasure principle—a basic tendency in each of us to strive to minimize pain and maximize pleasure. The tendency is often at odds with reality, the truth about life as it really is.

We all know this feeling. How can we not when daily we see TV commercial proof that successful people take care of their problems in a flash? The lie says that when Mr. Average gets his plane flight canceled, he nonchalantly pulls out his gold card, saunters up to another counter, and hops on another flight. In reality, however, Mr. Average would probably have to spend the night in the airport.

The world is telling us that the more successful we are, the less troubled we are. The good life is the easy life, and if our lives aren't easy, we're obviously not doing well. We are already telling ourselves this lie so loudly and wanting to believe it so badly that when the world joins the act, we nod in happy agreement, convinced the lie has to be the truth.

But life is *not* easy, no matter how many gold cards and door openers we have. The very first words of the best-selling book *The Road Less Traveled* are golden: "Life is difficult. . . . Once we truly know that life is difficult—once we truly understand and accept it—then life is no longer difficult."[8] That is one of life's all-time great truths.

Remember Susan at the beginning of chapter 2? Susan was convinced that life was easy for everyone but her. Why did she get the rotten husband? she moaned. Why didn't she get the job she wanted? Why did her windshield get cracked? She was certain she was the only one in the world that had it tough. What was the result of her attitude? Bitterness. It's the response I see most often in my patients who live this lie.

Christians often embrace the Easy Life lie with open arms, and they are, ultimately, the ones more susceptible to future bitterness. Many believe that a real Christian will have a carefree, "rose garden" life. If not, they wonder if their faith is really real. Christ, shortly before his crucifixion, while offering a special kind of comfort and help to handle it, warned his disciples that things would be anything but easy for them. "In the world you will have tribulation," he said. "But be of good cheer, I have overcome the world."9 We tend, because of our Easy Life lie, to hear only the comfort and not the warning.

I think one of the best promises that Christianity offers is "all things work together for good to those who love God, to those who are the called according to His purpose."10 And it's something we need to understand while coping with the "rose garden" lie. God doesn't promise there won't be any misfortune or trouble in our lives. He does promise good can come out of bad, but only with struggle and difficulty to realize that final good.

True Christian living demands tremendous sacrifice that hurts. Christianity clearly requires a "face the pain" lifestyle, which is probably one of the main reasons so many people avoid it altogether or only allow themselves limited involvement once they realize the truth. Along these lines, I love Wilburt Rees' comment: "I'd like to buy $3 worth of God, please. Please, not enough to explode my soul or disturb my sleep, but just enough to equal a cup of warm milk or a snooze in the sunshine. . . . I want ectasy, not transformation, I want the warmth of the womb, not a new birth. . . ."11

Life is not easy. Life is tough. The willingness to face problems, accepting the truth that life is strewn with them, is paramount to a life free of bitterness and confusion. Susan was right about one thing. Some people do have it better than she does. Some people, many people, though, have it worse.

The other day, Susan came to our session smiling. She sat down with a plop and said, "Dr. Thurman, I had a wreck yesterday."

"Really?" I said. "Are you all right?"

She said, "Oh, yes, I'm okay. It was a fender-bender, but you know, the woman in the other car jumped out screaming, 'Why does this always happen to me! I can't take anymore of this!' She went on and on, and as I stood there watching her, I forgot all about my bent fender for a moment. All I could see was that woman. She was 'me' all over! I suddenly understood that everybody else feels the same way I do. And better, I can choose how I'm going to respond to things like that. I really can."

Susan's emotional well-being rested on whether she could exchange her Life Should Be Easy lie for the Life Is Difficult truth. With such growing awareness, I'm glad to say she has, and much of her anger and bitterness has subsided. The old lie "tape" still plays occasionally, but the new truth "tape" is playing more loudly and strongly; her emotional state has made a dramatic turn toward health.

"Life Should Be Fair"

"Hey, that's not fair. Your piece is bigger than mine. Mom!!"

"Chris, share with your brother. Be fair."

Fairness is taught us in the schoolyard, in the classroom, and especially at home if we grew up with brothers and sisters. In retrospect, though, this kind of upbringing, where everything is as fair as possible, has turned out to be both a good and a bad thing. It was good in that it molded character and showed us our parents cared for us all equally. But it was bad because it may have fostered a belief that life would be always fair, which it most definitely is not. I'm only half joking when I say I wish my mother had, on occasion, given my brothers and me unequal pieces of pie with the explanation, "Hey, we love you guys all the same, but life ain't fair sometimes, and we want you to learn that truth early."

This fair-life offshoot of the Easy Life lie is just as pervasive and just as potent. It's wishful thinking, and it's damaging. A young man is killed by a drunk driver. A less qualified applicant gets the job. The front-runner is tripped by another runner and loses the Olympic gold medal. Our response is, "It isn't fair," as if labeling it could put it right. Solomon, thousands of years ago, understood life's unfairness when he wrote, "There is a vanity which occurs on earth, that there are just men to whom it happens according to the work of the wicked; again, there are wicked men to whom it happens according to the work of the righteous."[12]

Several years ago, a friend's father had a heart attack and could not run his drug store alone, so he hired a young pharmacist to manage the store until he could come back. The young pharmacist embezzled $40,000 of drugs and money to feed his own drug habit and then was caught. If that wasn't bad enough for my friend's father, right after the young pharmacist made bail, the store mysteriously caught on fire. Nothing could be proved, so the insurance company paid for the renovations, and the store opened for business six months later. The next month it burned again. This time, the insurance company said they would pay this time, but they would not renew their coverage. And without insurance, my friend's father would not be able to stay in business, a business he'd had for thirty years.

Not fair, we all yell. Not fair at all. There are drug dealers who are multimillionaires, murderers who escape punishment on a technicality, governments who kill those who speak out. And yet we still expect life to play fair!

Of course, life isn't always unfair, either. Saying so would be just as big a lie. The spark of the divine in us all often wants to play fair and expects others to do the same. But what we *expect* is the problem. My patients who are driven by this lie, who harbor decades of resentment, have only one resource to become emotionally well. They must strike a balance here for healthy truth.

Lee Anne is a good example of this balance. During the fifties, she grew up in a southern family where the men were favored, subtly and not so subtly. Her parents sent her brother to prep school, paid his way through an expensive eastern college, and set him up in his law practice. For Lee Anne, public school was good enough. She made valedictorian, after all. She'd do fine. Then they offered tuition at a nearby state college. "My father said I'd just get married anyway," she commented.

"I believed it all myself until I was in my midtwenties," she explained. "My brother naturally deserved the best. Then suddenly it all hit me, and I was livid. It wasn't fair. I was just as smart, even smarter probably. Yet he was 'the man.'"

What could she do to get rid of the resentment, especially since her elderly parents still catered to her brother?

The balance must come from a bit of rational, reality-based self-talk, as we mentioned earlier (and will delve into deeply in our How-To section). First, I agreed with her. The whole situation was unfair. I pointed out that though it was a reality, it was a past reality.

"What do you mean, a past reality," she said. "I still feel it."

"You're making a past reality your present problem. You're reliving that past right now, aren't you?" I said.

"Well, yes," she hesitated. "But what is this balance you're talking about?"

"The grossest unfairness is to keep yourself paying today for something in the past," I said, "because psychologically that's where you still are."

Lee Anne thought about that for a second, gazing out the window, then responded, "You're saying, it's not in the past as long as I keep reliving it?"

"Right," I said. "What's the worst thing you can keep doing? What would be doubly unfair?"

She was beginning to understand. "If I keep reliving it, if I let it keep bothering me," she answered, "the past stays unfair, and I'm wrecking my present." With that kind of self-talk, Lee Anne was better able to step out of the victim's role, keep the past and the present separate, and cope with current realities better. It's up to us to handle unfairness so as not to pay twice for it—once when it happened and once when we allow it to wreck our lives now.

"Don't Wait"

Elaine loved clothes. She always looked as if she stepped off the cover of *Vogue* when she came to see me. But that love is the very reason she comes to see me. Elaine, an overspender, is deeply in debt. She seems unable to stop herself from buying everything she sees.

"I did it again," she said. "I bought a dress I didn't need. I just couldn't resist. It was the most beautiful thing I'd ever seen."

"You felt you couldn't live without it," I ventured.

"Right. Even though it cost $450, I had to have it."

"Didn't you tell me last session, you'd charged your cards to the limit?" I asked.

"Yes, but one of my cards upped my limit, saying I was a good customer," she said sheepishly.

"How do you feel about what you've done?" I asked.

"Happy but guilty. I know I shouldn't have bought the dress, but I'm happy. I look great in it."

Earlier, we talked about the You Can Have It All lie. The Don't Wait lie is a variation on the same theme; its falsehood stems from the same impulse. You can have it all, so why wait? Why not have as much of it as you can *right this very second*! Whip out that credit card; shortcut that degree; don't hold back on that impulse to tell that person off who offended you.

Most of us know the lure of instant gratification in small daily ways. We really shouldn't have those greasy, calorie-laden French fries with our hamburger, but what the heck? We only live once. We'll start that diet tomorrow. Why wait?

I find out pretty quickly which of my patients live by this Don't Wait lie. They come for help thinking that psychologists have magic words that will instantly make their lives free from pain. Once they see that therapy is going to be long, difficult work, some simply don't come back. These patients come to therapy to be immediately changed by the psychologist, not to change themselves.

Why wait, indeed? Today we are living longer than any generation in history, yet we feel more rushed. Time seems shorter, not longer. Waiting is not anyone's idea of the perfect life. Recently, I read about a government study that found that only two cents of each dollar earned in America is being put into savings—an all-time low. In other words the average person only puts 1/50th of what he or she earns into that "delay of gratification" tool called a savings account.

Of all people, Christians should understand waiting. The importance of waiting on God is almost stamped on every page of the Bible. It speaks of putting off pleasure on earth for long-term reward in heaven. It says,

> Wait on the LORD;
> Be of good courage,
> And He shall strengthen your heart.

It warns not to store up "treasures on earth," but delay gratification to heaven.[13]

Yet I have as many Christian patients prone to the life of immediate gratification as anyone else who comes to my office. That may stem from the fact that Christians live in the world just like everyone else, and they listen to the same worldly lies. Why? Because, as I mentioned before, they want to. The lies sound good. The lies even can meet our needs on a short-term basis. It's the long term that lets everyone down. Elaine found this out during one of our sessions.

"So," I continued, "you wouldn't feel as good about yourself if you couldn't wear that new dress?"

"This one will make me stand out! All heads will turn!!" she said, grinning, eyes shining.

"Do you think you are caught up in how you look because, underneath it all, you are starving for love and attention?" I asked and waited for her reaction. Her eyes quit shining.

"Well, I don't know. I've always wanted to look good," she said, automatically straightening herself into an elegant pose.

"For whom?" I asked.

"For everybody. For myself!"

"Okay. And why do you think you need to look good?"

She cocked her head toward me. "Are you saying that all this spending comes from my wanting to be loved and admired by others?"

I shrugged and waited.

"I mean, that could be true. I guess everybody wants that," she said.

"Yes, but not everybody goes into debt for it. You've made your credit card your best friend."

She laughed. Then suddenly she quit and frowned thoughtfully. "Okay, I know what you're saying. But what should I do when I want to use my 'best friend'?"

"What do you think?"

"Come get you."

"No, I don't think so. What we *can* do here is help you redefine what your basic needs are and start to talk about meeting them in more appropriate ways. For now, though, what can you do when you want to spend? Give me a couple of ideas."

She thought a second. "Maybe I leave my best friend at home? I guess that would be a start."

I agreed and waited for her next suggestion. Elaine was starting to understand.

"People Are Basically Good"

Amy, an attractive twenty-five-year-old computer programmer, has been seeing me lately to try to sort out reasons for her series of bad relationships with men. She is a bright, articulate, and responsible woman whose life is under control, except for one area. Every relationship she has had with a man since she was a teenager has been chaotic and painful.

"I just don't know what keeps causing my relationships to go bad," she said one day. "I end up feeling used and hurt every time."

"When you date a man, what assumptions do you make about his intentions?" I asked her.

She looked a bit startled. "Assumptions? Well, I don't know. I guess I assume he's like me."

"What do you mean?" I asked.

"I assume his intentions are that he wants to get to know me for me and see if a relationship can develop."

"Honorable intentions, then?" I said.

"Yes, honorable."

"Specifically, how do you see them being honorable?" I asked.

She smiled, a bit chagrined. "You know what I mean. That the guy is moral. That sex isn't the only thing on his mind. That he likes my company."

"And what have you discovered?" I asked.

She grimaced. "That most men are out for themselves. They don't care who they hurt."

Amy's problem isn't so much that she is choosing the wrong men. Obviously, she's doing that. I think her basic problem is her underlying assumption that men, and people in general, are basically good.

Does it sound strange for a psychologist to suggest that believing people are, by nature, good is a lie?

In an age when *human potential* and *self-actualization* are buzzwords and when best-selling books include *Being Your Own Best Friend* and *Looking Out For Number One*, the idea that our nature is flawed tends to threaten us because it forces us to give up cherished notions about our own goodness. Many of us prefer to accept more positive or humanistic views of human nature. For example, here is the view held by noted psychologist Abraham Maslow:

> This inner nature, as much as we know of it so far, seems not to be intrinsically or primarily or necessarily evil [but rather] neutral . . . or positively 'good.'. . . Since this inner nature is good or neutral rather than bad, it is best to bring it out and to encourage it rather than to suppress it. If it is permitted to guide our life, we grow healthy, fruitful, and happy.[14]

This view of human nature certainly makes us feel better, but is it true? I don't think so, and I can point to three main sources of evidence that the scales of human nature tip toward evil.

First, on an interpersonal level—people interacting with people—the history of humankind is marked by greed, hatred, conflict, and murder more than self-lessness, love, and peace. The holy wars and the Spanish Inquisition are good examples of warping good itself toward evil. The holocaust and the threat of nuclear war in our own century are enough to make my point.

Second, on an intrapersonal level—within ourselves—humanity seems bent individually toward self-destruction as much as growth. Physically most people do not exercise enough or eat a balanced diet. Emotionally most people are plagued by some degree of turmoil, often severe enough to require professional help. Mentally, people often have faulty ways of viewing themselves, others, and life in general. Spiritually, most people do not seek God or any form of meaning in life with much consistency or depth. In fact, many feel that life doesn't really have much purpose to it at all.

Third, I believe that the Bible teaches that we are corrupted by a sin nature, which will ultimately destroy us if it is not brought under control by God himself. "The acts of the sinful nature are obvious: sexual immorality, impurity and debauchery . . . hatred, discord, jealousy . . . selfish ambition, dissensions, factions and envy; drunkenness, orgies. . . ."[15]

Not exactly a great picture of what our basic nature is like when it is not yielded to God, is it? I want to make it clear, though, that I don't agree with those who say we are *totally* evil and incapable of good. History also supports how loving and kind and noble people can be. We are created in God's image, and so we mirror his qualities too. We *are* capable, then, of tremendous good and tremendous evil, but as I see it, we are bent toward evil.

Fine, you are probably saying, but what does that have to do with lies? The understanding of the human tendency toward evil, the acceptance of the bad as well as the good within us, is fundamental to a healthy trip through life and life's relationships along the way.

So many of my patients are casualties of the People Are Good lie. Like Amy, their expectations of those around them are the highest and purest, when a healthy skepticism would serve them better.

"Is it wrong to think the best of people?" Amy exclaimed when I suggested a healthy skepticism to her.

"Well," I said, "it's not proving to be true, is it?"

She stopped, a bit startled, then shook her head. "That's for sure." She sighed. "But what's the alternative? Should I assume all guys are scum and not trust anybody?"

It was my turn to shake my head. "That sounds like going to other extreme."

"Yes, I guess so."

"What would be a middle ground?" I asked.

"Well, let me think," she said, shuffling her feet and looking down at the carpet. "Maybe I should hold off my conclusions." She looked back up at me. "I mean I can't really know about the guy's intentions until I check them out."

"So you wouldn't *think* either way?" I said.

She nodded. "I wouldn't assume they are good or bad. Right? In fact, I wouldn't assume, period. Maybe I wouldn't reveal so much so quickly either. Maybe I'd study the guy a little more."

"And how would that affect your dating life?" I asked.

"I'd pace my relationships slower. I wouldn't be so totally naive." She paused for a second. "I trust too quickly, don't I," she said, more of a statement than a question. "They can't use me unless I let them; I know that. So I should work on patience, on letting the relationship go slow."

Amy's decisions, I'm glad to say, have not only made a dramatic change in her relationships with men but also with everyone else she knows. She tries hard not to assume anything at first. Either drastic belief—that people are totally good or totally bad—is equally destructive. A moderate approach to those around us, where we see others as capable of good and bad and needing help from God to avoid being ruled by evil, is the truth I present to my patients. It strikes me as the most balanced approach to ourselves and others.

HOW TO DEFEAT YOUR LIES

Now you know some of the lies the world teaches you. Obviously there are many more, but these are the ones I hear most often in my work and the ones you'll most likely be battling. At the end of chapter 2, I introduced you to the ABC approach to help you clearly identify which of the self-lies you tell yourself. You need to continue your ABC journal, adding any of the worldly lies you believe.

As you do, though, I want you to take a step further. I told you in chapter 2 that monitoring your emotionally troublesome lies was enough to tackle for the moment. Now that you have been practicing the ABC approach in your journal (You *have,* haven't you?), it's time to correct these lies. The next move to defeat your lies involves challenging those lies—by extending the now-familiar ABC approach. We need to add two steps, a *D* and an *E*.

Actually, it's quite simple. If you recall, *A* stands for the situation that triggered your emotions, *B* stands for the "self-talk" of lies or a mixture of lies and truth through which you interpret the event, and *C* stands for your emotional response. The new steps can be explained easily:

D—is *truthful* self-talk. Consciously, you'll engage yourself in this kind of self-talk, which will counter the lies you tell yourself at *B*.

E—is the more appropriate emotional response, given what happened at *A*.

See? It's simple. Remember the example we used to learn the ABC approach? Let's add the *D* and *E* steps to it.

A—*THE EVENT:* Standing in the express checkout line, you became irritated, frustrated, and angry at a woman in front of you who was taking her sweet time. The lies you told yourself at *B* were: "I can't be happy unless this line speeds up." "The woman should be . . . (more perfect)." "Her taking so long is making me angry." These need to be countered with the truth:

D—*TRUTHFUL SELF-TALK:* To defeat those lies, you can tell yourself any or all of the following:

"I can be happy, even when things don't go my way."

"People are people. They often don't do things as perfectly as they could."

"Getting all bent out of shape doesn't make the situation better. It only makes it worse."

"She isn't causing my anger. I am causing it by virtue of what I am telling myself."

"I don't like being slowed down. But it's not the end of the world."

Do you see how telling yourself these truths over and over in your head at the time of the event can put a lid on an emotionally troublesome situation?

E—The correct response would then be a more calm reaction. You'd understand that you are causing your own strong emotions, so you can also calm yourself down to a healthier level now that you're telling yourself the truth about your situation.

Okay. Let's try another one, using the whole approach:

A—*THE EVENT:* You have an appointment with your doctor at 3:00 P.M. At 4:00 P.M., you are still waiting in his tastefully appointed waiting room.

B—What will your normal self-talk be?

C—What is your immediate emotional reaction?

At B, you probably tell yourself something like: "Hey, this isn't fair. I got here on time. Why can't he be on time?" Now, think—what lies are you telling yourself with these statements?

• Life should be fair.

• Things have to go your way for you to be happy.

• People should be perfect.

Of course, I can already guess what your C reaction is. While biting your nails and thumbing through back issues of *National Geographic,* you can rehearse the lies you are telling yourself and you can keep getting angrier and angrier. *Or* you can use the truth to help calm you down and resolve your explosive emotions. Let's try to add step D to your situation. What truths can you tell yourself to counteract your angry lies?

D—*TRUTHFUL SELF-TALK:* "I don't like waiting

like this for my doctor, but getting *overly* angry about it only makes it worse."

"My time is just as valuable as his, but he is good at taking however much time he needs with all his patients—who include me."

"I do dislike waiting. But whether I like it or not, that's what I'm doing. I can choose to be miserable or do what it takes to help me resolve my feelings of anger. What can I do?"

"I can spend my time doing something constructive, maybe start a letter I've been meaning to write, maybe think about something pleasant, maybe bring a book next time, maybe see this as free time to let my mind wander."

Now, what would the response at E be?

The challenge in adding steps D and E to the ABC situation is to take the truth and use it as a weapon against your lies. Don't worry if your initial efforts result in less-than-immediate improvement in your attitude or emotions. Your lies will always be hard to change, given how long you've practiced them.

Think of the lies you believe as your native language. The truth, then, is a foreign language with words that are sometimes hard to pronounce and remember. Just as you can learn a foreign language with enough effort and practice, you can learn to speak fluent truth. Patience is the name of the game here, once again. Truth doesn't come in a jingle, but the truth will create emotional balance and well-being if you give it time and practice.

MARITAL LIES

To understand the realities of the marital relationship it is essential first to recognize the unrealities.

William Lederer and Don Jackson[1]

Joe and Carol had a storybook romance. He was handsome and attentive. She was stylish and smart. They became engaged and expected to live happily ever after. Then they got married. And instead of happily ever after, they were living unhappily all too soon. Where Joe once seemed handsome, Carol now found him vain; where he once seemed attentive, he now seemed possessive. As for Carol, she no longer seemed stylish and smart to Joe, but materialistic and know-it-all. Soon they were fighting in a big way. And have been ever since. Two nice people who were very much in love turned into two unhappy people wondering if they had made a big mistake.

What happened? Nothing that couldn't happen to any couple. Reality moved in. When Joe and Carol married, their romantic notions of life together came straight from fantasy land. When real life didn't live up to their dreams, troubles ensued.

For many, many reasons, most couples begin their

lives together believing a lot of lies. And when the truth finally comes, either they find enough love and hard work to adjust, or they cling to the lies until the marriage slowly crumbles.

Marriage is hard work. Now that's a truth. Yet blinding romantic notions let us ignore it until the very last possible moment. Many couples live through heartbreaking pain and misery. But I've noticed that almost all the couples I've counseled have voiced ideas reflecting a pattern of lies, which are largely responsible for their marital misery.

Keep in mind that these lies we'll be discussing are not lies most married couples would consciously admit to believing. Rather, the lies affect them on an unconscious level, which makes confronting the lies much more difficult.

"It's All Your Fault"

One of the most frequent lies that couples engage in is a form of the It's Somebody Else's Fault lie, which points the finger of blame squarely at the marriage partner. It implies that the actions of one spouse make the other spouse react in a bad way and are the only things making the marriage rotten. Simply put, it's all his or her fault.

This was Joe and Carol's problem from the first moment of their sessions with me. Joe sat with his body turned away from Carol, Carol with her legs crossed away from Joe. And they began. . . .

"She never says anything nice about what I'm doing," said Joe.

"That's because you never do anything nice. All you do is come home from work and complain how awful it is and how much you hate it," Carol answered.

Joe shot back, "If I got a little more understanding from you, I might not complain so much."

Carol sat up, indignantly. "So here we go. It's all my fault you complain so much, is that it?"

"If you'd listen more and be less critical, I wouldn't complain as much," Joe said.

"Yeah, well, if you didn't complain so much, I could listen better," Carol countered.

They had played this verbal volleyball all their married life. They admitted they had argued like this for fifteen years, and neither seemed willing to back down and look at his/her individual contribution to the problem. When I tried to open their eyes to how they personally needed to change, how they needed to look at themselves honestly, they became defensive and accused me of taking sides.

Do you remember the old cliché, "It takes two to tango"? It really does! It takes two people to create a horrible fight and two people to create a horrible marriage. Even when it seems that one person is clearly the only one "messing things up," I still would argue that the "offended" spouse's response to what the other spouse is doing is just as important to marital harmony.

If, for example, Mrs. Jones tells me one afternoon that she just spent $1,000 on clothes, whether or not they get into a destructive fight would hinge as much on what Mr. Jones does as on what Mrs. Jones did. Mr. Jones could respond hatefully to what she did, or he could respond with concern and see if Mrs. Jones would be willing to undo what she did. In other words, he would have a choice in deciding how to respond to her actions (even though he'd probably have to have you remind him of this fact at the time). His choice of response to what she did is just as important in determining marital harmony as was her decision to spend $1,000.

Here are some ways he could respond:

The Put-Down Response

"Are you telling me you spent $1,000 on clothes in one day?" he yells. "That is just like you! All you think about is yourself. You don't give a darn about our finances and how your spending affects them. You are nothing but a selfish brat!" he blathers on.

Mrs. Jones' response, like anyone else's is to blather back defensively, if, that is, she doesn't run out of the room, slamming the door.

The "Keeping the Peace" Response

"Uhmm, well . . . that's great! I'm glad you found what you wanted," Mr. Jones mumbles as he grips the kitchen counter hard enough to break a knuckle.

Mrs. Jones' response, though, might be, "Good! Tomorrow I'll go and get those other things I put back."

The "Speak the Truth in Love" Response

"I'm glad you found clothes that you like," Mr. Jones says, setting his briefcase down, and turning straight to her, "but I've got to tell you, I think $1,000 is way too much to spend, given our budget. Let's talk about this."

Mrs. Jones' response? If he has made a habit of such reasonable responses she might answer like this: "I will be happy to discuss this with you. I want both of us to feel good about how much I spent."

Obviously, the third response is the healthiest one. No blame is being thrown around, and Mr. and Mrs. Jones are still communicating. It may sound somewhat idealistic, but I think communication like that is possible between couples if they work hard enough.

In a more serious case, Patty had an alcoholic husband who verbally and emotionally abused her. She was convinced that their marital problems were all his fault, and, frankly, he was the instigator of most of them. She had no self-esteem left, she felt humiliated in front of her friends, and her children were embarrassed about their dad's alcoholism. And they no longer had a father they could depend on. It was all his fault, she'd say. All. But I reminded this woman that while her husband was responsible for his alcoholism and the abusive behavior it led to, she was responsible for whether or not she let his actions wreck her life. And that, unfortunately, was exactly what she was doing.

Finally, in one of our sessions, she blurted out the "truth" she was living by:

"Until he quits drinking I can't be happy," she said, looking at me angrily.

I waited a minute, then responded: "Don't you think that's a pretty high price for his alcoholism?"

She sat up. "What do you mean?"

"Well," I went on, "as if his alcoholism wasn't problem enough, you seem to be willing to add your own personal unhappiness on top of it."

She looked indignant. "Well, it seems to me that being married to an alcoholic husband who verbally abuses me doesn't leave much room for happiness."

She thought I couldn't argue with that. There was all the truth of the world in her statement, it seemed. Yet part of it was the lie of her utter helplessness to control her own response. So I said, "I agree that it makes life more difficult, but you seem to be building a case for making it the crushing blow that dooms your life to misery. Does that really have to be?"

"I don't know. I guess not, but . . ." she stopped.

"Patty, you're in a bad situation. There's no doubt about that. But you can make a decision: Do your husband's actions have to doom you to unhappiness?"

She sat staring down at the floor, then finally answered, "I don't want it to. But I just can't see how I can be happy unless he quits drinking and putting me and the kids down. He always says we're holding him back, smothering him."

"Could you be smothering each other?"

"Maybe," she mumbled. "Sometimes I feel I'm choking to death."

"Your decision is whether you can commit yourself to being your own person, enjoying life anyway. Think a minute. How can you do that?"

She looked past me a moment, then said, "I . . . I've thought of separating from him, maybe . . . for a while."

"And how would that help things?"

"It would hurt, but maybe it would wake him up. I don't know. It goes against everything I've been taught. But things get so bad sometimes . . ."

"Are there other things you could do that would help you be more fulfilled?" I added.

"Well, actually, I've let lots of my friendships go because I was . . . well . . . so embarrassed. I feel so lonely sometimes. I used to like to quilt. I don't see my quilting friends anymore. And I quit going to church altogether because I couldn't look anybody in the face."

"Beyond embarrassment, what's stopping you from starting those relationships back up?"

"Nothing, I guess," she said. She smiled a little, and I noticed a bit of life in her eyes.

Being content in spite of circumstances—that's a great goal. Easier said than done? You bet. But that doesn't make it any less our responsibility. When the Day of Judgment comes, I honestly don't think that God is going to tell her, "Look, you had it really rough being married to that bum of a husband, so you are off the hook for how you reacted to him and how you let his alcoholism affect your life." Instead, I think he'll be more likely to say, "Look, you had a husband who acted horribly, but you were still responsible for how you handled his actions and whether you allowed his problems to ruin your life." We don't have control of how others treat us, but we must take control over our own actions and reactions.

As much as is humanly possible, couples need to take to heart the biblical teaching to be honest about our own flaws and work on them before presuming to take swipes at those around us—even those with problems as serious as Patty and her husband's. As Matthew so picturesquely puts it, we should make a point of looking at the plank in our own eye before we point out the speck in our spouse's eye.[2] We cannot allow the speck in our spouse's eye to make our plank larger and more blinding. Can you imagine a marriage in which each spouse puts this one teaching into practice?

"If It Takes Hard Work, We Must Not Be Right for Each Other"

Back at the beginning, this chapter says marriage is hard work. Make that: Marriage is *very* hard work. *Tremendously* hard work. Underline it. Boldface it. Tattoo it to your forearm. This is the first rule of marriage: Any marriage that stays healthy and happy through the years has been *worked* on. It's a truth, though, that very few understand. So the moment the marriage isn't smooth, couples begin to wonder: "Are we right for each other?" The idea seems to come from another lie—that there is someone in the world with whom we could live "happily ever after." This is what happened to Carol and Joe, our "storybook romance" couple.

As strange as it sounds, I'd argue that hard work in marriage often suggests you married the right person (although I realize there are exceptions). Overall, the difficult struggles in our marriages often show us where our own personalities are deficient and give us the chance to clean up our act.

Lately, I've been seeing a couple in therapy that fits this scenario. Cheryl and Dan have been married less than a year and fight about something almost every day—large things, small things, anything. They have few interests in common and feel bored with each other. They spend little time alone talking about how they feel because they find it hard. And their attitudes have spilled over into their sexual life, which is sporadic at best. They'd call it quits except that they're afraid of being single and of how their friends and family would react.

Typically, they blame each other and wonder if they're hopelessly wrong for each other. I've tried to coax them to back off each other and look honestly at their own personal styles.

When they see me, they habitually sit in the two single chairs in my office, a king and a queen sitting regally, rigidly in their individual spaces—Cheryl, self-assured and immaculately dressed, Dan slouched and always in slacks and a rumpled sport shirt.

"I know how frustrated you both must be with the problems in your marriage," I said one day, "but I don't think they necessarily mean you are wrong for each other."

"What else could all of our problems mean?" Dan shot back.

"Well, one thing they could mean is that both of you have flaws to work out in your own personalities. The fights are just a symptom of how much work you have to do."

Dan rolled his eyes. "C'mon. How could a flaw make us fight?"

"Dan, you mention how much you like watching sports, but you do seem to go overboard at Cheryl's expense," I ventured.

He stiffened. "I love football. It helps me relax. You are going to ask me to give that up?"

"Of course not. It's not my place to ask you to give it up. It's more whether you think it should be cut back some to help your marriage. It's got to come from you."

"You're asking the impossible with him," Cheryl mumbled. "Look, don't you think we both could find someone else we could get along with more naturally, not work so hard?

"I'm sure there are people out there who would be better matches for both of you," I admitted. "I don't think that means that your marriage needs to be shelved to go find them. The odds are you'd end up marrying someone who wasn't better for you at all, maybe even worse. The painful truth is that marriage helps to bring out the areas of our lives we need to work on. You'd just be taking the same flaws into your next marriage. Divorce is just a quick fix."

Cheryl and Dan both stared at me when they heard the word *divorce*. I had no doubt they wanted to talk about it, fall back on it, anything to take the easy way out.

"My personal belief is what I can share with you," I went on. "I believe that maximum personal growth is found in your own marriage. The pursuit of a 'new, improved' spouse is usually an escapist fantasy." And with that, I noticed neither of them was looking at me anymore.

For the time being, they are considering this notion. Their pain is so acute, their anger so intense, I worry they'll divorce before the work they need to do is started, much less finished. But I constantly remind them that their problems signal not that they should leave each other but instead that they need each other's help to work out the unhealthy aspects of their individual personalities.

Unfortunately, marriage therapy is often like my work with Dan and Cheryl. Before I can help them come to the point of working on their individual problems, couples sometimes destroy the marriage through yelling and screaming over each other's faults. A "change or else" decree rarely works. In fact, it often makes things much worse because people, spouses included, don't like to be threatened or manipulated into changing who they are.

Our first couple, Joe and Carol, have this problem, too. And they are both Christians. In fact, Christian couples seem all too prone to this particular lie. "If it takes hard work, we must not be right for each other" seems true to Christian couples because, at some level, most Christians think God would not have allowed them to get married if the marriage was going to be a difficult, painful one. The "God brought us together" feeling many Christian couples experience leads them to finish the thought with "therefore, we will always be happy with each other." This flies in the face of biblical teachings on the difficulty all marriages encounter. Paul says in 1 Corinthians, "But those who marry will face many troubles in this life, and I want to spare you this."[3]

Marriage is very hard work. We are better off not using that truth as an excuse to bail out of the marriages we are in.

"You Can and Should Meet All My Needs"

Another unrealistic notion many of us have is that someone out there will completely, totally, consistently, and wonderfully meet our every need. We meet this "perfect" person, marry, then all too soon begin to notice the person's "gaps." And still we cling to the notion. You'd be amazed at how stubbornly some people hold on to this idea. I've seen couples in my office who've been married thirty years and are still hanging on to the idea that their spouse should meet every wish, want, and desire. Lies die hard!

George and Sue came to see me after their tenth anniversary. They had hardly celebrated it at all because they realized how unhappy they were with each other. George was the analytical type, an engineer. Sue, just the opposite, was bubbly, the cheerleader type, who had always had someone "stronger" come to her rescue. She even admitted that George was her Prince Charming, just the way she had pictured her father before he died. George always paid the bills, called the repair service, handled every little car problem. But lately it had begun to drive him crazy.

"She expects me to do everything!" he blurted.

"I do not. I just expect him to be there when I need him," Sue answered, all reasonableness.

George sighed. "Do you realize what you're saying? You're saying, 'Here's my life; take care of all my needs!' I can't do that! Nobody can do that!"

"Oh, George, I don't expect you to do everything, just what I can't do. That's what husbands are for," Sue joked.

"Sue, this is serious. Listen to me. I can't keep my own life organized sometimes, much less yours," George almost yelled.

Sue frowned, looking intently at her husband. "But," she began, "if you don't help me, who will?"

"Maybe that is an important question to face," I said to Sue. "Who will take care of your problems and needs if George can't or won't?"

Sue's eyes began to look a bit scared. "Well, I don't have friends or family to rely on, like George does."

"How does that make you feel?" I pressed.

She paused. "I guess I feel afraid. To hear George tell it, I always run to him. Well, maybe I do. Maybe too much. If he wasn't there . . ."

"Maybe you're running from your fear of independence," I suggested.

"I have to admit," she said in a quiet voice, "that when we first met, George wanted to meet all my needs, and I wanted to let him. I needed a refuge."

"That's true," George added. "I wanted it then. It made me feel important and needed. Now I just feel smothered and used by her needing me so much."

"I hear you saying, George, that the ground rules have changed," I said, "and that Sue doesn't know it. Sue, is that right?"

Sue thought a moment. She straightened her dress and crossed her legs. "I think George isn't as willing to help me as he used to be. I think maybe I need to learn how to take care of myself a little better. I need his help to teach me." And she looked at George.

"George?" I said.

"Of course!" he brightened. "It's not that I don't want to do anything, honey. It's just I can't do everything anymore."

The reality of any relationship is that no one person can be the perfect "need meeter" for another person, so our needs are best met through a variety of healthy, appropriate sources. Many people who tell themselves this lie are ones who don't have these healthy sources—a best friend, hobbies, satisfying work, or even a solid relationship with God.

So rather than identifying this lack as the problem, they will turn to their spouses and say, as George put it, "Here's my life. You take care of my needs." It's a nice, crisp way to avoid taking responsibility for making one's own life full and complete.

Also, I say healthy, appropriate sources because it's all too easy today for a marriage partner to try to meet those unmet needs in unhealthy, even adulterous, ways—ways that will in no way help the marriage.

Tom is a good example of this. To put it simply, the lie Tom believed was that his wife wasn't "perfect" enough for him. So he went out and found other women to meet the needs his wife wasn't meeting. To be frank, his primary "unmet" need was for sexual variety, and since his wife couldn't change shape and form to provide him a different visual stimulus each month, à la the *Playboy* Playmate of the Month, he went looking. Of course, this lie helped to ruin their marriage. He ignored the fact that he wasn't perfectly meeting his wife's needs and his selfishness ultimately damaged their relationship, perhaps irreparably. He's now moved out of the house, and his wife and children are without husband and father, all in the name of his getting his needs met "perfectly."

I can hear you now: "Hey, I don't expect my spouse to meet all my needs. I'd be delirious if he/she just met some of them!" To be honest, I've known couples in which one partner was definitely the more deficient one in meeting the basic needs of the other. Tom is a good example of that. He ignored his wife's need for fidelity, for companionship, for help in parenting. Other spouses may be faithful sexually but ignore needs just as important without realizing what they are doing. Understandably, the spouse whose needs aren't being met feels the "give-get" equation is way out of balance. In those situations, I tell the "wronged" spouse that it's critically important not to blast the deficient partner. In being "swift to hear, slow to speak, and slow to wrath"[4] the wronged spouse can give the "deficient" spouse a chance to examine why he or she resists being a better spouse.

Basically, the challenge here takes three forms: 1) to examine honestly what you expect from your spouse, 2) to examine honestly whether he or she can or will meet those needs, and 3) either to get the need met in an appropriate way through some other means or accept that the need is inappropriate and work to give it up.

For example: One of the problems of our original couple, Carol and Joe, is that Carol loved antiques, and she wanted Joe to go along with her when she shopped and browsed. Joe, on the other hand, saw every antique as a piece of old furniture and worried that all Carol's purchases would soon make the inside of their house look more like his great-grandmother's house—which he never liked! He certainly did not want to drag along behind Carol as she rummaged through warehouses of musty old dressers and tables. Obviously, since Joe hates what Carol loves, she could better meet her need by finding others who love antiquing. Expecting Joe to have all the same interests as she did was unrealistic, and she needed to let go of it.

No one person can meet all our needs. Our spouses need to be let off the hook if that is what we are expecting from them.

"You Owe Me"

Remember when you first started dating your spouse? You were glad to do things for him or her and didn't really want much in return, other than his or her company.

What's your relationship like now? If you're like most couples, you have developed a "green stamp" marriage style. For everything you do for your spouse, you build up a certain number of green stamps in your mind. Taking out the garbage might be worth ten green stamps, picking up the dirty clothes might be worth fifty, listening to complaints might be worth seventy-five, and doing with him or her something you don't want to do is worth a hundred green stamps. Then, when you feel the need, you dump out your barrel-load of green stamps and say, "Here, I want to cash these in for a trip to Hawaii" or "You owe me three hours of your undivided attention— NOW!"

For some reason, maybe because familiarity really does breed some contempt, we go from our dating years (when we did things out of desire with little sense of what we were owed in return) to our "stuck with each other" married years (when everything is totaled up for payback).

This "you owe me" marriage style is destructive and is rooted in the lie that people, specifically our spouses, pay us back for everything we do.

Melissa and Burt epitomized this lie. They constantly had their "radar" up for what the other person owed them, and they got very hostile toward each other when they felt they were "paid" less than what they were owed. It had become so bad that they were never at peace with each other. Our sessions revolved around and around the "you owe me" theme until finally, one day, we came to an insight that triggered a slow turnaround in their marriage:

"Look," said Burt, leaning toward me, "I've worked so hard to give her everything she wants, and all I ask in return is to do some of the things I want to do."

"You feel like she owes you that, huh? For what you've done for her?" I asked.

"Yes, I do," he said, leaning back.

Melissa almost exploded out of her chair. "Well, what about all the things I've done for you? What do you owe me?"

Burt crossed his arms. "Like what? I bring home all the money."

Melissa began counting on her fingers, "Helping put you through graduate school, keeping house and putting dinner on the table every day, paying all the bills so you don't have to mess with them, raising our kids all alone while first you studied and now you work. NEED MORE?"

"Wait," I said. "Both of you sound convinced the other owes more than you do. Okay, then. Burt, whose efforts are worth more, yours or Melissa's?"

"That's not fair. Nobody can decide that," Burt said.

"Exactly," I said. "How can we ever honestly know what our spouse's contributions are really worth?"

Melissa said, "What do we do?"

"You tell me," I said.

Melissa answered, "Well, I think we first need to do a better job of dividing the work that needs to be done around the house. For my own peace of mind, I need to know we are sharing the load as equally as possible."

"And . . . ?" I asked Melissa.

"And then quit worrying about who owes who what. If we can," she said.

Burt ran his fingers through his hair a couple of times, then sat back in his chair. "Yeah, I can live with that. We can try it anyway," he finally said.

Try to imagine a radically different approach to marriage. What if you take the point of view that your spouse owes you absolutely nothing for all the things you've done for him or her? You have done what you have done in the marriage because you chose to, not because you had to, and no one owes you anything for doing what you chose to do.

Take it another step. What if you take the point of view that when your spouse does anything in return for what you've done for him or her, it is because *your spouse* has chosen to, not because your spouse has to. And what if you look upon what your spouse offers you as something to be accepted and appreciated instead of *expected*?

What I am proposing is this: Marriages get a lot healthier when you give up your expectations of each other and replace them with wants that, if not met, you meet in other ways.

Please keep in mind that I am not suggesting that in giving up our expectations we should quit *wanting* or *desiring* things from our spouses. I *want* my wife to be loving, remain faithful, help me around the house, and keep a balanced checkbook. I'm just suggesting that she doesn't *owe* me those things, even if I meet *her* expectations. The minute I start demanding these things from her as if they were my marital "birthright," I am believing my lie tape and will quickly fail to appreciate what she does offer me.

You might be saying, "Okay, let's assume I quit expecting my spouse to meet my needs and just start wanting my partner to meet them. What do I do when my spouse doesn't give me what I want?"

Well, you have a number of options, some healthy and some unhealthy. On the unhealthy side, you can yell and scream, withdraw, demean, manipulate, or intimidate your spouse into giving you what you want. You may actually get what you are after, but you have won the battle and lost the war because your style will create ill will and a lack of love and harmony in the marriage.

On the healthy side, you can *ask* your spouse to reconsider, or you can flex a little, compromise, give up wanting it, or, if all else fails, go take care of it yourself without being bitter. The truth is that spouses "owe" each other nothing in marriage. The healthiest marriages are those in which each spouse gives because it is right to do so, not because it was owed or in order to be owed something in return.

"I Shouldn't Have to Change"

When I was a teenager, a song I loved had a line in it that went, "I am what I am and that's all I ever will be." I hear couples say this very thing in defending why they can't (or won't) change.

"I've always been this way and can't do anything about it. If you really loved me you would just accept me for what I am and not try to change me."

Of course, the main thrust of these statements is the lie that in a good marriage spouses don't have to—or shouldn't have to—alter who they are for each other. It's as if a wife should just say, "Well, that's just my husband and I love him anyway," and move off into some twilight zone of blissfully accepting the unchanged version of him.

What malarkey! *Of course* we need to change who we are to fit our spouses better. The challenge is deciding *what* to change. When we marry, all of us have aspects of our personalities that are deficient and need to be tuned up or overhauled. More often than not, our weaknesses are our spouses' strengths. Marriage involves improving our weaknesses, not wrapping ourselves in an "accept me as I am" flag.

My wife, Holly, has a tremendous capacity for emotional closeness and intimacy; I tend to be more analytical and emotionally distant. During the early years of our marriage, I often felt uncomfortable when she would want closeness—say, a simple hug, for instance—and I didn't feel like giving it. This was very frustrating for both of us. To be honest, I wished at times that she would just accept me as I was and not expect any more emotional intimacy than I wanted to offer.

I remember one time when she just wanted to hold my hand. I had had a draining day full of meeting other people's needs. At that moment, all I wanted was some personal space. I didn't want her to hold my hand. I didn't want her to be mad; I just didn't want to be around anyone. But in my gut, I knew that what Holly wanted was right and that I needed to change. In other words, I knew my problem with emotional intimacy was a flaw in my personality. I knew I needed to be as open as possible to her, especially when she reached out to me. It hasn't been easy, but I'm trying to break past my own fears of intimacy with her help. I may or may not ever be as comfortable with emotional closeness as Holly is, but her influence is making me a much more complete person.

"One flesh"—that's what Genesis calls a married couple.[5] Becoming "one" is impossible if one or both spouses refuse to change for each other. I'm all for individuality, and I don't condone blind conformity to whatever a marriage partner wants just to make him or her happy. But when my wife is strong where I am not, it makes sense for me to move in her direction as much as I can. And vice versa, of course. With that kind of mentality, both of us win because both of us become more complete—while we are becoming "one."

"You Should Be Like Me"

This lie is a second cousin of the previous lie and is much like the "My Way" lie mentioned in chapter 2. The belief is that your own personal style is the "best" style and that your spouse must think, feel, and act like you in order to be right or acceptable. People who fall into this lie tend to see the world in black/white, right/wrong, all/ nothing terms. They often arrogantly assume that because they think or act a certain way their spouses are wrong if they don't believe and act the very same way. In blunt terms, such people want more of a clone than a partner, whether they see it that way or not.

Carol and Joe, our original couple, believed this lie, and it was one of the many misconceptions causing their marital misery. They both felt that their own personal view on any issue was the best, smartest, wisest, and most accurate, and when they clashed, they clashed in a big way. For instance, one year Carol "knew" that a vacation to the beach would be best for them and had all the logical reasons to back it up. At the very same time, Joe had decided that a vacation to the mountains was the best choice, and he had just as many good reasons. Unwilling to back off their opinions, they spent countless hours arguing the topic. Finally, they were so mad at each other, they didn't go on vacation at all.

This seems absurd in print, but I know many, many couples who make this lie a lifestyle. In fact, if we were married to someone who felt and acted exactly as we did, we'd be bored within a week. I'm not suggesting that couples avoid pursuing their personal preferences just to avoid arguments. I am suggesting that we ask ourselves if the preference we have is important enough to fight over. If not, we need to be flexible enough to compromise or give up what we want at times.

We are unique. It's good that we are all different, even if it does lead to conflict, because maturely handled differences can give us a clearer sense of our own individuality and a greater appreciation for how different human beings really are.

Marital lies are usually ones you deny, unconscious ones that'd make you squirm if brought to light. But deep down you probably know you have some of these on your own tape recorder. Marriage therapy, when properly done, involves making these lies conscious and then replacing them with the truth, an action you are capable of beginning yourself. One of the best tools I use in marriage therapy is the next How-To we'll discuss.

HOW TO DEFEAT YOUR LIES

Let's try a totally different How-To: "rational-emotive imagery"—a mental game developed by Dr. Maxie Maultsky, a leading proponent of cognitive restructuring therapy and used by athletes for years to prepare for competition. We'll be using it for some of the important situations in our own game of life.

Put simply, this How-To involves imagining an unpleasant or disturbing situation and using truthful self-talk to change the emotions associated with it.

How would an athlete use this technique? Picture a tennis player who has been missing the back corner, game after game. He is sinking into negative thoughts: "I'm lousy. I'll never put the ball away. I just can't do it." Instead of giving up, though, he stops himself cold and decides to try imagery.

In his mind, he plays out a situation in which he misses the corner again, but this time he stops the action, backs up, follows through again, and mentally puts the ball exactly where he wants it. While imagining this, he tells himself, "You can do it," "Keep at it," and "All it takes is concentration." Then he continues to do it over and over in his mind until the idea becomes something he begins to accept as possible.

Let me give you an example using me as the subject:

THE INCIDENT: I have a suit I need dry-cleaned for an important meeting tomorrow. I can't drop it off myself this morning, so I ask my wife to do it for me. I make it crystal clear how important it is that I have this suit by tonight. When I get home, though, my dirty suit lies exactly where I had left it this morning.

MY BAD REACTION: I do not handle this situation well. I explode. I tell myself several different lies at this point:

"This is horrible! I can't wear anything else to the meeting! My whole day is ruined, not to mention the rest of my night."

"I can't depend on my wife for anything! Can't she do anything right?!"

"This is all her fault! And look at all the things I do for *her!*"

At this moment, my wife unfortunately enters the room. I let her have it, and we have one of the worst fights in the history of our married life.

Now, let's imagine the same scenario but with different mental and emotional outcomes.

MY IMAGERY: I walk in the door and discover my rumpled, dirty suit exactly where I left it this morning.

This time, though, I tell myself the truth in one of the following ways:

"I'm very disappointed she didn't do what I asked. There's nothing I can do about it now, so I need to figure out what else I can wear to the meeting tomorrow."

"She said she would take care of this. Sometimes she doesn't do what she says she is going to do, just like I don't always do what I say I'm going to do. I don't like it, but that is reality."

"This doesn't *have* to wreck my evening or the meeting tomorrow. I will handle it the best way I can."

"When I see her, I will tell her I'm upset that she forgot my suit, but it's not the end of the world, so I will keep my wits about me."

While I am thinking these rational thoughts, I imagine myself feeling relatively calm about the situation. I imagine that I am angry but in control. I imagine that I talk to my wife and tell her I am upset about the suit, but I am doing it in a way that is respectful and "hearable." Last, I imagine myself letting the issue drop and going about the business of finding a solution to my suit problem, instead of wasting time placing blame.

(Of course, some of you will say that this is all very nice, but jumping up and down is the only way to make sure that your spouse knows how important this was and to help him/her remember to do it right *next* time. My response would be that that style creates a vicious circle, a "cry wolf" situation. You've jumped up and down so often that your spouse hardly notices, and so you've trained him/her to ignore you when you really mean it. My answer to your statement, then, would be that you have to break the cycle, informing your spouse that you are doing so and sticking with it. If this is your situation, you will need this imagery How-To more than you'll know to break this old habit.)

The rational-emotive imagery technique allows you to take normally explosive situations and mentally play them out in reasonable and constructive ways. You can visualize handling the situations well. In a sense, the technique gives the brain a motion picture in which you practice doing your "scene" long before your actual "performance" or after a bad performance so you can work on doing it better.

In fact, this technique can be used to help defeat lies that would harm you in all types of situations. You can use it to prepare for job interviews, confrontations with friends, saying no to unrealistic demands, coping with mistakes that you or others make, handling your children's misbehavior, or getting through a demanding day. As with all our techniques, don't be discouraged if you're not good at imagery at first. With practice, you'll become quite skilled at allowing the truth to seep visually into any situation and work its wonders on your coping mechanism. The challenge is seeing yourself handling the situation badly, then, as the tennis player did, putting the mental tape in reverse and imagining yourself handling the situation well.

5.

Distortion Lies

The less clearly we see the reality
of the world—the more our minds are
befuddled by falsehood, misperceptions, and
illusions—the less able we will be to determine
correct courses of action and make wise
decisions.   Scott Peck[1]

When was the last time you blew up over something small?
Do you find you take things far too personally?
How often do you use the words *always* and *never*?

Do you feel first and think later?

Be honest. How did you answer those questions? Each one concerns a distortion. In our perceptions, we often distort reality. That practice is the foundation for most of our lies. Some of those distortions are quite familiar in themselves, and they foster their own familiar false ideas.

These distortions and the lies they fuel are:
- Magnification—the Mountain out of a Molehill lie
- Personalization—the Taking Everything Personally lie
- Polarization—the Black/White lie
- Selective Abstraction—the Missing the Forest for the Trees lie

109

- Overgeneralization—the History Always Repeats Itself lie
- Emotional Reasoning—the Don't Confuse Me with the Facts lie.[2]

I've seen people use these distortions in thinking over and over to warp daily events and conversations out of truthful proportions.

The truth, of course, is that everybody does it. Everybody is so guilty of such distortions that they have become part of most people's normal thinking. Each one of them, though, contributes to the lie mentality and needs to be exposed through our lie point of view. Let's look at them one by one.

"A Mountain out of a Molehill"

Jill dragged in her front door. It had been a very, very long day. Nothing had gone right at work. As she opened the door from the garage, she glanced into the den. The place was still a wreck from her son's football-watching party the night before.

"He promised!" she said at the top of her voice.

At that inopportune moment, her son walked in the door.

Jill exploded. "You promised! You promised me this morning you'd do those dishes before you went to work! That is all I need to see after a day like this! I'm sick and tired of your defying me! After all I do for you! You are grounded for a month!" And then, leaving her son standing speechless, she stomped off to the bedroom, slamming the door behind her.

Jill is suffering from the distortion called *magnifica-*

tion. In this distortion, an event is made much bigger than it is in reality. Like Jill, the person makes a mountain out of a molehill. By taking what her son did (or didn't do) and making it into a bigger situation than it really was, Jill was lying to herself. And, by lying to herself, she turned up the volume on her emotions.

Odds are you've been through a scene like this. The tendency to magnify is one of the more common ways to distort reality. We often take five-cent events and turn them into situations we consider much more valuable, valuable enough for the emotions they evoke. (The flip side of magnification, taking an event and minimizing its importance, is equally unhealthy.) But the emotions don't fit the situation. The more we magnify, the more emotional we get.

I have a horrible time keeping my cool in traffic. Someone's failure to give a turn signal, as small as that is, can "yank my chain." Given that it is impossible to go out on the highway without seeing someone doing something "wrong," my tendency to magnify can make driving a frustrating and anger-provoking experience. What do I usually end up doing? I point my finger at the offending motorist as if he is the real culprit for the feelings I am having, rather than seeing my tendency to magnify as the real reason I'm so downright irritated.

Life in general has thousands of five-cent irritations like traffic, hundreds of fifty-dollar events like not getting a raise, and far too many five-thousand-dollar tragedies like the death of a loved one. Total these events and you get a very difficult life. A person who takes each event and multiplies it into a more costly event makes his life almost intolerable. None of us is built to cope with a life that feels that big all the time.

So how could Jill have handled that "breaking point" mess? Her best option was to realize she was "magnifying" at that moment. When you feel like wringing somene's neck, recognizing a distortion is hard to do, but recognition is more than half the battle. After recognizing she was "making a mountain out of a molehill," she could then try to determine the true size of the events and react accordingly. Easier said than done, no doubt, but worth the doing for her emotional health and her relationship with her son.

"Taking Everything Personally"

"He comes home late every night from work," Cindy was saying in one of our sessions. She and her husband, Paul, were seeing me for marriage counseling.

"Why do you think he does this?" I asked her.

"It's obvious," she said, folding her arms, hugging herself. "He comes home late because he doesn't have the least bit of respect for me. He doesn't want to be with me. He doesn't love me anymore."

Cindy's reaction to Paul's lateness is a style of distorting called *personalization*. In this distortion, the person overestimates the extent an event is related back to him or her. *Everything is personal.*

We all do it, don't we? Whether the initial event is someone's looking at us in a funny way or cutting us off in midsentence or forgetting an appointment with us, we often will interpret the action as a deliberate intention to hurt us or slight us.

Couples tend to personalize quite a bit. If the husband leaves his dirty socks in the middle of the floor or drinks too much or never wants to talk, the wife takes it personally. If the wife is always gone at night to committee meetings, if she never takes anything he says seriously, if she never wears that perfume he likes so much, the husband takes it personally.

I'm not suggesting that we should react with indifference to what our spouses do or that their behavior is totally unrelated to how they feel toward us. I'm only suggesting that our tendency to personalize makes us overreact, which makes the situation worse. Not only is the original problem still intact, but we add unnecessary anger, resentment, and bitterness to the mess.

Cindy felt Paul was neglecting her by always coming home late. That was the bottom line of her personalization lie. She viewed his tendency to overwork and his habit of ignoring her as a direct reflection of how he felt about her. His workaholism incensed her. I responded to her as I respond to most of my patients who personalize such a problem: "Cindy, could there be other reasons for his continual lateness?"

She frowned, "I guess it's possible, but I sure can't think of any offhand."

"In any given situation, let's assume there are at least four explanations for someone's behavior. Try to name four things that might cause Paul's lateness beyond that he thinks poorly of you," I said.

She sat silent.

"Cindy, at least try," I finally said.

She made a face. "Okay. I guess he could just have a problem with being late. He always did, you know. But it was always just a few minutes, not hours and hours."

"Good," I said. "That's one."

"I suppose he could be wanting to impress his boss."

"That's possible," I said. "His job could easily be such an extension of his self-esteem that he's become a workaholic to feel good about himself."

"Mmmm," she answered. "Maybe."

"How about a third one?"

"He doesn't know how to say no," she said, teeth clenched.

"That could very well be true," I said. "Especially if his job means a lot to him. And the fourth?"

She looked me in the eye. "He doesn't want to be home with me," she said defiantly.

"C'mon, a fourth that has nothing to do with you. Does he have trouble with intimacy?" I asked.

"Well, yes, he does. He never talks about his feelings. I always have to pull everything out of him."

"His lateness could be that. Intimacy could be scary for him. He may feel safer at work where he's in control. So he stays there later and later."

She pursed her lips, then nodded. "Maybe. But I still think he doesn't want to be home with me."

"That can be a self-fulfilling prophecy, you know," I said. "If you react hatefully to his workaholism because you are taking it personally, if you yell and treat him badly, he may begin to think of you and home in the very way you don't want him to. And he might stay at work even longer."

Cindy didn't reply, but it was obvious from her face she understood all too well the truth of what I said. Of all the explanations for Paul's lateness, she chose the only one that had to do with her personally. The possibility that his lateness had nothing to do with her never really crossed her mind.

Wait a minute! you might be saying. Paul's workaholism is insulting to Cindy, and she *should* be mad at him for neglecting her! Of course, there's some truth in your righteous indignation.

Think of it this way, though. If Cindy stays mad at Paul and uses hate and anger to get him to change, do you think he will? If he does, do you think it will last?

In my experience, situations like Cindy and Paul's

don't get better until hurt feelings are eradicated, until the focus is more on who Paul is—what makes him do what he does—than how it affects Cindy personally. Almost without exception, when the discussion turns to alternative reasons for the other person's behavior, the patient begins to see that he or she is not the true reason for the other person's actions at all.

Instead of personalizing every little thing that happens to us, then, we need to stop and ask a very important question: Is what the other person did a statement about what he or she is like? Or a statement about what I'm like? Or a little of both?

No matter how badly we are treated, we don't have to take what has happened to us as a 100 percent reflection of who *we* are. If someone rides my bumper in traffic, I can interpret the action as, "That guy has little respect for me!" or I can interpret it as "That guy has little respect for other drivers of whom I happen to be the current one he is being disrespectful toward." This may sound like splitting hairs, but these two views create totally different emotional responses. The first is like a slap in *my* face. The second is an observation of who the other person is—a person with little respect for others—and the emotional response to that bit of truth is much more reasonable.

It reminds me of a quotation I love: *At age twenty, we worry about what others think of us. At forty, we don't care what they think of us. At sixty, we discover they haven't been thinking of us at all.*

The next time someone swerves in front of you on the highway or forgets to call you back or leaves the newspapers all over the couch, try to remind yourself that, generally speaking, what other people do says much more about them than about you. How *you* react to them, though, says a lot about who you are.

"Black/White"

"Everything is so black and white to you!"

Ever had this criticism thrown your way? If so, you are being accused of a style of distorted thinking called *polarization,* which takes reality and cuts it into black and white—all or nothing—extremes.

If you polarize, you often find yourself reacting to things with either a "That was great!" or "That was awful!" gut feeling. At home you run the vacuum in straight lines and get angry when your spouse runs it in curlicues. You lump people into good guy and bad guy categories. Politicians, for instance, either elicit your admiration or your loathing. This style of thinking doesn't even allow you to see the greys of life, much less appreciate them. And when turned inward, such polarized thinking brings severe emotional fallout.

One of the more serious "inward" forms of polarized thinking is "scum/saint" thinking. Many of my patients view themselves as either completely scummy or completely saintly, or they flip back and forth between the two. Along these lines, I recently read an interview with the actor Daniel J. Travanti, best known for his portrayal of Captain Furillo on the television show *Hill Street Blues.* When asked about his struggle as a young actor with alcoholism, he described himself as having been an "egomaniac with stong feelings of inferiority." Basically, he was saying that he flipped back and forth between feeling like a scum and feeling like a saint. He probably turned to alcoholism as a way to numb the pain of such emotional highs and lows.

I would be less than honest with you if I said that people never behave in scummy ways. I'd also be lying if I suggested people never behave in saintly ways. The fact of the matter is that most of us act both ways at times. But we distort reality when we see only the extremes in ourselves and others.

To label ourselves as "scum" or "saint" or to stick either label on others is to miss seeing the whole person. When aimed inward, the label of "scum" breeds nothing but low self-esteem and depression, while the label of "saint" breeds arrogance and "holier than thou" feelings.

The "saints" are an interesting group. I have had hundreds of people in my office who never in their wildest dreams had thought they would do the things they did. The truth about ourselves is that we are capable of doing almost anything. The "saints" do not—cannot—believe this truth. When they "fall" then, they simply are in shock about the "impossibility" of their actions. Usually it takes a tremendous amount of work to help such people see the arrogance behind their assumption that they are too good to do such things.

Though she'd never admit it, Sally saw herself as a saint. All her life she'd played the role of the "good girl." She grew up in the church and was taught a strong value system, so she became a highly moralistic adult, an avid church worker, and a well-known civic leader. Since Sally was seen as such a good role model, she was constantly being asked to work with youth. She even chose a somewhat selfless line of work—she administered a church-sponsored charity.

Two years ago, if you'd asked Sally if she would ever commit adultery, she would have either laughed or sniffed indignantly. Yet that is exactly what she did. She had been friends with a man at her office for years. One night she and the man were working alone at the office after a grueling but successful fund raiser, and the unthinkable happened.

"How could I have done this? How could I let this

happen?" cried Sally in one of our first sessions. How could she be a scum? That was what she wanted to ask. How could she, of all people, commit such a sin?

"I feel so dirty. I've come this close to suicide!" she said, holding her thumb and forefinger a quarter of an inch apart. "How could it have happened?"

"Tell me about your marriage. You're married, aren't you?" I asked.

"Yes, I'm married. To a good man. What else is there to tell?" she said, looking down.

"How long have you been married?"

"Fifteen years," she went on, fiddling with the pleats in her skirt. She paused a moment, then continued fiddling. "My only gripe with him is he's not very affectionate. He doesn't like to touch much. He's a whole lot like my father in that regard. He really is a good man, though." She finally looked up. "This would kill him. He trusts me implicitly."

"When was the last time you were affectionate with your husband?" I asked.

She stopped and thought. She shook her head. "I can't tell you. Isn't that awful? I guess I gave up after a while." She gazed at me, "But that doesn't make what I did right, does it?! Me of all people! How can I go back to work? How can I look anybody in the eye—especially if it gets out!"

She of all people is the exact thinking that helped trip her up. Such arrogance is the perfect example of Solomon's "Pride goes before destruction." Why? Have you noticed that if you know you're weak in an area, you're more careful of it? For instance, what if you were a weak swimmer? Wouldn't you wear a life vest or be more careful in water? Often, those who drown are those who overestimate their own swimming strength.

Perhaps a better analogy would be your car's blind

spot—a point where the sideview and rearview mirrors miss what's coming behind you. If you know your car has a blind spot, you don't trust the mirrors as much. You turn your head to see what's coming.

Pride can set the stage for committing sins because you aren't watching your blind spot. You're saying you don't have one. That's exactly what happened to Sally. Going all the way back to her father, she had a need for male attention and affection, which was not being filled. She had done as many women do; she married a man much like her father, and so her need for affection had to be filled elsewhere. She filled it with civic work; she filled it with youth work. She filled it with activities that brought her praise. At a moment she didn't see coming, though, she filled it in an unacceptable way—with a man whose company she'd enjoyed for years. Her need overcame her strict moral sense. And she didn't even see it coming.

Would it surprise you if I said that arrogance also underlies the conviction that you're much worse than everyone else? The claim still implies a uniqueness about yourself. It is the equivalent of saying, "I am such a uniquely *horrible* sinner that I stand out above all the rest of you mediocre sinners." Both lies, scum and saint, involve a faulty, distorted belief in one's own unique goodness or awfulness, neither of which fits reality.

Obviously, there are certain issues that *are* black and white, and we need to view them that way. The existence of God, for example, is a black-and-white issue in my opinion. He either exists or he does not exist. Jesus Christ, then, was either God Incarnate or he was not. Sins against society such as murder or stealing are also black-and-white matters. I don't think we can afford to be grey about them.

The polarized thinker, though, takes all of life and

forces it into a black or white format. When the issues faced are black and white, there is no problem. When the issues are grey, though—as many are—polarized thinking creates needless anger and hurt. The challenge is to be flexible enough to read the "shade" of a situation properly, reading black as black, white as white, and the in-between as its appropriate shade of grey. We need to be able to use good judgment and discern issues a "shade" more accurately.

"Missing the Forest for the Trees"

An offshoot of the Polarization lie is one called *selective abstraction*—the "can't see the forest for the trees" distortion. Do you ever focus on a small thing to the exclusion of all else? For instance, have you said something fairly goofy in a crowd at a party and spent the rest of the night worrying about your remark?

Leigh, a friend of mine, had just gotten a nice promotion. The promotion, though, involved some added pressure she wasn't sure she could handle. One day I ran into her, and I could tell she was upset.

"I blew it! I know I'll lose this job," she exclaimed. "You should have seen it. There I was, at this fancy restaurant with my boss and a big client. And what do I do but drop my fork. I mean, I don't just drop it; I fling it! It made a big stain on my dress and then bounced about fifty times on the floor. I couldn't speak above a mumble the rest of the meal."

She went on like that for another ten minutes or so. Finally, I said, "Leigh, come on! Nothing *nice* happened?"

"If you call laughing 'nice.' That's what the client did. He said, 'Don't you worry about it.' And then he called the waiter over and got me another fork."

"And?"

"And we got the contract, but I bet my boss won't trust me again in a situation like that."

"Leigh, it sounds like everything worked out fine. You might even have humanized the whole meeting."

"What?! How? I just can't agree. It was awful!"

In spite of all that had gone right, Leigh could only focus on the one thing that had gone wrong. I helped her see her "selective abstraction" lie and what it was doing to her emotionally. Since that time she has worked on defeating this lie in her life, much to her own emotional betterment.

As a university professor, I used to teach an introductory psychology class with an enrollment of about a hundred students. During my lectures, I would often scan the auditorium and notice the students who were not listening to my lecture. Some of these students looked bored, others were talking to their neighbors, and still others looked semicomatose. Out of the hundred students in front of me, the students not listening may have made up 5 per cent of the class, yet I would often catch myself focusing on these students to the exclusion of the 95 per cent who were paying attention. I'd end up feeling anxious and depressed about myself as a professor. My own "forest for the trees" problem made me feel bad about something that was really a positive in my life.

Many psychiatric patients are in the hospital because of their tendency to focus on what is wrong with who they are, rather than on what is right. It's as if they have on a pair of "deficiency" glasses, which allow only the bad to come through. When you only see the bad, depression is close behind.

It isn't hard to find examples of this in everyday life. A person may work hard all day, only to remember what he or she did wrong rather than what was done right. A housewife may spend a tremendous amount of effort to clean up her home, yet when the day is over, she only sees the things she didn't do. A tennis player might hit ten good shots and miss one and then only think about the miss. A parent might ignore a child when the child is behaving and only pay attention to the child's misbehavior.

I have seen some Christians use selective abstraction when they read the Bible. Selective abstractors may only pay attention to verses that have to do with judgment or sin or works while ignoring verses on grace or forgiveness. (Of course, there's also the opposite distortion: remembering only the promise verses and disregarding God's caution that life can be difficult.) Selective abstractors often have a "green letter" edition of the Bible, the kind that has all the doom and gloom verses highlighted with green felt-tip pen. Would you be surprised that these Christians usually end up much more anxious, fearful, depressed, and guilt-ridden than those who are able to see the "whole" of the Bible?

Whether this "missing the forest for the trees" style of thinking affects how we look at our own personality, the behavior of others, or the teachings of the Bible, we waste an amazing amount of our precious time and energy doing it.

"History Always Repeats Itself"

Larry was coming to see me for his weight problem. He was an obsessive eater. He'd eat when he felt bad, which led to despair, which led to eating, which led to fatness. Some cycle!

"I'm never going to be able to stop this," he moaned. "I'll always be fat. Let's face it."

Notice the two key words in his statement? *Never* and *always*. These two words are the keys to a style of distorted thinking called *overgeneralization*. In this distortion, any event or behavior, like eating a Twinkie, failing an exam, or fighting with a spouse, leads to the lie that the future will inescapably hold more of the same. History, supposedly, *always* repeats itself.

It isn't uncommon for many of my hospital patients to overgeneralize about their mental health. They often fear that they will never get better. When they conclude this, they typically keep up the same, self-defeating styles of thinking and acting that made them ill in the first place. My response is to push them to see each day as a unique opportunity to turn events around. They often fight me on this, but it would be very difficult for them to improve when they are feeling doomed to repeat the mistakes and pain of the past.

Overgeneralizing is also a favorite style of thinking for married couples. "We will never get along with each other," couples conclude, for instance, and then they fall back into the same old patterns of criticizing and nitpicking, which, in fact, ensure they will never be happy with each other. When this prophecy fulfills itself, the couples say, "See, I knew we would never get along!" Therapy is always a struggle for such couples. It's almost as if they'd rather be right about their overgeneralization and miserable than wrong about it and happy.

"Larry," I said to my overweight patient, "let me ask you something. In the last few years, have you had to learn some new skill?"

"What do you mean? Like learning that stupid computer at work? I thought it would kill me," he said, rolling his eyes. "I would never have even started trying to learn how to operate that crazy thing if my job hadn't been on the line. Took me forever."

"Okay," I said. "Did you think before you started that you'd never be able to work the computer?"

"Are you kidding? I didn't even know how to type!" he exclaimed, throwing up his hands. "I knew I was going to be demoted."

"While you were trying to learn it, did you think you'd ever learn?" I asked.

"I thought I'd *never* get it," Larry groaned. "The first month was a killer. A thousand times I thought of giving up and packing it in."

"You thought you'd never handle it. You thought you'd always be a computer illiterate. You thought it so much that the task seemed to grow into a mountain. Every day you just knew you'd fail, but every day you kept trying, right?" I coaxed.

"Well, yeah, that's what happened," Larry agreed.

"And then what happened?" I asked.

He shrugged. "I learned it. Gradually, it kicked in, and I started understanding it, and now I handle it just fine."

"You broke through that overgeneralization, didn't you?" I said.

Larry, a bit surprised, smiled. "Yeah, I guess I did." Then, as if a light bulb went on in his head, he looked sideways at me, and said, "And now you mean I can break through this one too?!"

"You did it once, didn't you?" I pointed out, as I watched Larry getting used to the idea.

Although he continued off and on to tell me his eating problem was different, Larry and I both knew that his argument was hollow. He couldn't ignore the fact that he'd overcome a supposedly impossible problem once, and he knew that meant he could defeat others. After a few weeks, he began coping better with his overeating. The simple truth Larry found out was that the cards we are dealt (or deal ourselves) don't have to be the cards we end with. That *F* on the first exam doesn't have to be the grade at the end of the course. That bad start with a co-worker doesn't have to turn into a bad relationship. *Always* and *never* don't have to take up permanent residence in every discussion of our future. History doesn't always have to repeat itself. We *can* change.

"Don't Confuse Me with the Facts"

"I'm worthless," Angela said to me one day in our session together. Angela was an attractive woman in her late thirties who'd been divorced ten years ago and was now considering remarriage. "I know I'll screw up this new marriage, like everything else I do. I tell you I'm worthless."

"Prove it," I blurted out, much to her surprise.

"How far back do you want me to go?" she said caustically. "In high school, I lied to my best friend about going out with her boyfriend. I did that a lot. In college, I did drugs. And I not only kept lying about going out with my girlfriends' guys, but I slept with the guys—not with one or two, but with a whole college full. Then I flunked out of college. Then I got married to this guy I didn't love because he had money, and when I got tired of him, I started running around with other men until he divorced me. Shall I go on?"

"That sounds like ancient history," I said. "Besides, all you've given me so far is proof that you are capable of doing wrong things. I want proof that you're worthless. Does doing wrong things make people worthless?"

"Well, no, not when you put it that way," she said, but I could see she was not completely convinced.

"Then why do you think what you've done makes you worthless?" I asked.

A little of the defiance went out of her manner. "I guess because I feel worthless. I did some pretty worthless things, you gotta admit that," she said.

Angela feels worthless; therefore, she is worthless. That's what she said to me. Her response is a perfect example of *emotional reasoning*. It is a distortion which says, "Because I feel it to be true, it is true." Usually, this is not a distorted style of thinking that we openly recognize. It is masked by other lies, making those lies *feel* like truths. In Angela's case, her emotional reasoning was fueling the I'm Only as Good as What I Do lie, for instance. Emotional reasoning can make feelings appear to be facts.

Feelings, though, are just feelings. They change quite a bit, they are hard to predict, and they often spring from irrational and unrealistic ways of thinking.

Hopefully, you can see that feelings often yield unreliable assessments of what the "facts" are. In our culture, though, we almost *worship* feelings. "If it feels good, do it" is just one of the ways we justify making feelings the ultimate criterion for a decision.

What would your life be like if you did nothing but follow your feelings? If you're like me, you'd buy everything in sight, shoot people for cutting in front of you on the highway, and run off to the Bahamas. A feeling-based life would be, at best, chaotic.

I am not suggesting that feelings should be ignored. Feelings give life a lot of its richness and spice, and they certainly need to be seriously considered in decision making. But they shouldn't be the only consideration.

Take someone who is deciding what job to accept. If he or she just relied on feelings, he or she might not ask some important questions to determine significant facts: Am I qualified for the job? Does the job allow for advancement? Do the current employees enjoy working there? A good judgment on any issue depends on both facts and feelings.

Think about your important decisions. Were they dominated by your feelings at the moment? The facts? Or a combination of both? Were the feeling-based decisions better than the ones made on facts? Or vice versa? I think you will find that decisions, major and minor, are much better when they are based on both your head and your heart.

Sometimes couples considering marriage come to my office and evoke my concern that they are making their decision on the basis of feelings alone. They say: "We love each other so much! We can't imagine having any problems!"

I often feel like saying, "Well, imagine it because it will happen. Once the velvet gloves come off and the glow dims, you'll wish you hadn't let your feelings dominate your choice."

In my premarital counseling sessions, we spend time looking at who the two people are: Do the two communicate well? Do they resolve conflict properly? Do they have a lot of interests in common? Has their becoming a couple made their spiritual lives stronger? The cold, hard facts that emerge have to guide their feelings if they don't want a bumpy marital ride.

Unfortunately, when people turn their feelings into facts, they become much harder to help. Angela, for example, had turned her feelings of worthlessness into fact, so she had locked herself into a position that made helping her almost impossible. After all, who can argue with "facts"? She had let what she'd done become the "whole" Angela—all of her. Her performance equaled her worth. So I tried to approach her problem from that perception.

"Angela, how do you feel when you do well?" I asked.

"I still feel bad," she answered.

"Isn't doing well just as much an indication of who you are?"

"What do you mean?"

"You seem to be easily convinced you're bad," I said. "I want you to consider an idea. Are you sure you don't *want* to feel bad?"

"Now *wait* a *minute!*" she said, almost rising out of her chair. "Why on God's green earth would anyone in her right mind want to feel bad?"

"That's what I'm asking you," I said. "You feel bad, don't you? You won't forgive yourself for your past, and you've written yourself off for the future."

She sat back, looked blankly at me for a moment, then said, "If that's true, how do I change how I feel?"

"For starters, let your feelings just be feelings, not unalterable facts," I explained. "And get back to the truth of who you are and what you can be. Otherwise your feelings will make your self-image unalterable."

Angela's choice, like ours, must be to harness her feelings while she considers the facts. Otherwise she'll be a prisoner to her feelings and the lies they tell her.

HOW TO DEFEAT YOUR LIES

So far we've discussed three How-To's: monitoring your lies by the ABC approach; challenging your lies with the ABCDE approach; and using visual imagery to practice truthful thinking in stressful situations.

For this chapter, I want to offer two How-To's. The first is called Identifying Cognitive Distortion Patterns, and it uses the ABC approach to help you identify the underlying distortions in your thinking, exactly as we've discussed in this chapter. Record your daily thoughts using the ABC method as often as possible; then read back through them and attempt to pick out the cognitive distortions in your self-talk.

How will this help? You'll gain insight into the specific distortions you're most susceptible to. Once you see the distortions in your life more clearly you can use new "self-talk" (D) to list alternative, nondistortion explanations for things that happen to you. For example, if you constantly select negative things to focus upon at the expense of larger, positive situations, I'd want you to make your self-talk concern seeing the whole "forest," not just the decaying trees you're stumbling over.

Remember Larry, my overweight patient? He was convinced he could never change. History was doomed always to repeat itself. I suggested that Larry write down all such negative thoughts he had during the day. Then I asked him to review them at the end of the day and insert some written self-talk. Under each negative sentence, he was to write a positive one. He could draw from experiences in which he had overcome old habits, as he did by learning the computer. After only a few weeks of this therapy, his attitude had improved amazingly. He was beginning to notice his own distortion pattern and actually doing something concrete about it.

Keeping a journal and using what you write to gain insight into your own distortion patterns can help you reduce your own tendency to distort. That, in turn, will reduce all the unnecessary emotional disturbance each of them causes you.

This chapter's second How-To involves a process called Opposite Thinking. It is deceptively easy. You see, the lies you believe are often the exact opposite of the truth, so forcing yourself to consider the opposite of your lie can quite simply bring you closer to seeing the real truth in any situation. Let's look at its effect on one of my patients you've already met, and then you can apply this technique to one of your own lies.

Jim, my patient from chapter 2, told himself the "I Must Be Perfect" lie, if you remember. "People won't like me unless I'm perfect," he confessed to me one day.

"Jim," I said, "what might be the opposite of that belief?"

He did a double take. "Well, 'people won't like me if I am perfect.'"

"Now, which seems closer to the truth?" I asked.

He scratched his chin. "In my gut, I still feel people won't like me unless I'm perfect, but now that you mention it, I guess I can see that people might have a hard time liking me if I *were* perfect."

"Go on."

"Well, if I were perfect," Jim said, frowning in thought, "I guess people might be threatened by that. They might find it hard to be around me because I might remind them that they aren't perfect."

"Okay," I said, "Now answer this question: Whom do you feel most comfortable around—people who are trying to *act* perfect or people who are comfortable with the fact that they are imperfect?"

Jim shrugged and reluctantly answered, "I guess if I were honest, I'd have to say the imperfect ones."

"Why?"

"I feel more at ease. Like they won't be judging me as much as they would if they were perfect."

"So, how do you think others feel? Think they might agree with you? That maybe they like you, imperfections and all, because those imperfections make you easier to relate to?"

Jim shook his head at me and grinned sardonically. "I hadn't quite thought of it that way. I get the message."

Opposite Thinking led Jim to see his lie from a different perspective. Let's try it. Think of a situation that you magnify beyond all proper proportions.

"It was just horrible, awful, and catastrophic!" you might scream in response.

Now, think the opposite. What would you say? How about something like, "What just happened to me was small, insignificant, and unimportant."

In most circumstances, the opposite thought is closer to the truth. Opposite Thinking helps redirect our thoughts toward a balanced view of what happens to us in life. While the opposite of our lies may not actually be true either—in other words, what happened to you may *not* be totally small, insignificant, and unimportant—considering the opposite of your lie(s) will give you a better chance to put the event in proper perspective. Then you'll have the choice to react appropriately. You'll be the one in control, not your lie.

6.

Religious Lies

Our minds are stuck in a rut, a pattern of
thinking that is antagonistic to the will of God.
Successful Christian living depends on getting
out of that rut and establishing another one that
is characterized by biblical values and ways of
thinking.

Doug Moo[1]

iane is your "average" Christian.

When she was a child, her parents took her to church every time the doors were open. She accepted the "do's" and "don'ts" of Christianity easily, learning her Scripture lessons well. As she grew older, though, she found church less than exciting, more like a duty. Sometimes she even wondered if she was really saved. When she came to me, she wanted to talk about God.

"God feels so far away," she said during our second session.

"Tell me more," I said.

"Well," she frowned. "I feel that when I sin he hates me."

"So you feel his love for you depends on your behavior?"

"Yes, that's it, I guess," she said, "because when I don't sin, I feel he loves me very much."

133

"When you feel he hates you, what happens?"

She didn't answer for a moment, then she mumbled, "I hide from him."

I looked at her a bit quizzically.

She knew she'd have to explain, but she looked as if she didn't really want to. Finally, she said, "I mean, I won't go to church. I don't read my Bible. I don't pray. I avoid any contact at all with my gung-ho Christian friends."

"You pull out—is that it?" I said.

"Yes," she admitted.

I thought a second, then asked, "Do you feel better when you do this? Do you enjoy it?"

"No, not really."

I paused. She looked uncomfortable. I decided to ask her a very forthright question. "Diane, has your Christianity ever been enjoyable or a source of comfort?"

She looked surprised for a second. Then, with an expression of relief, she answered, "No, never!"

Diane is suffering from one of the most resilient types of lies we tell ourselves—a religious lie. Somewhere in her religious training, she's been taught an erroneous concept of God, and it has stayed to haunt her to the point of changing her behavior. The sad thing is her experience is not uncommon. Many Christians have misinterpreted what the Bible teaches and end up believing religious lies.

Why are these lies perhaps the most resilient of all the lies we believe? First, religious lies are usually taught as theological truths by people we trust in our homes and churches. I'm convinced that some of the worst lies are preached from the "pulpit," whether it is located in our local church or home. If you can't trust your home and church, whom can you trust? Lies like these that are practiced over and over again since childhood are usually deeply held and very difficult to let go of.

Second, these lies are taught to us as God's beliefs, so the typical Christian has an extremely difficult time giving them up. To do so means, it seems, to directly disagree with God. Not many are willing to do that. Christians are caught in the proverbial Catch-22. If they keep believing these lies (which they actually see as truth), they stay spiritually and emotionally troubled, but if they dispute the lies, they feel they're displeasing God. Either way they go, they can't win.

Religious lies *are* like other lies in several ways, though. Like other lies, they are emotionally damaging. And like other lies, they are rarely questioned. The Christian might know intellectually that such beliefs are untrue, but still keeps responding as if they are truth.

Religious lies go a step further than other lies, however, because they make spiritual well-being almost impossible for the Christian who lives by them. It's tough. Without spiritual well-being, how can we be whole? The first step, as always, is to acknowledge these lies, so let's look at the most common religious lies my patients express.

"God's Love Must Be Earned"

"Diane," I said, "why do you think you've never enjoyed your Christianity?"

"Would you enjoy it if you always felt you were trying to measure up and never making it?" she challenged me.

"No, I wouldn't. You know, what you are describing

is something a lot of Christians seem to struggle with, and it seems to stem from their view of God. How do you view God?" I inquired.

"I see God as a harsh judge who damns people to hell," she shot back.

"Where do you think that view came from?"

"My preacher back home. All he seemed to preach on was hellfire and damnation. I think my image of God comes largely from that."

"Was *grace* ever mentioned by your pastor?" I asked.

She laughed, a bit sardonically. "If it was, I can't remember. I just remember being very scared."

"Any other pictures pop into mind?"

"Well, yes," she said. "Of me as a kid, getting punished. My father was strict. He yelled and screamed at us a lot. He showed little, if any, compassion."

"And do you see God and Christianity the same way?"

"Well, yes. Isn't that what Christianity and God are all about? To keep us good, on the straight and narrow path?"

You probably see the problem in Diane's thinking yourself. She has been conditioned to think that God's love is conditional. Maybe her parents, especially her father, taught her that in subtle and not-so-subtle ways to keep her from misbehaving as a child, and the idea stuck. In our therapy sessions, Diane and I had uncovered many instances when her parents withheld their love when Diane made mistakes, but interestingly enough she could think of no specific time they overtly taught her that their love was conditional. What parent would? Perhaps she saw such an attitude in their actions and mixed that conditional love with their strong Christian beliefs.

For whatever reason, Diane has fallen into the trap

of believing that her actions affect whether or not God loves her. The worse the sin, the more God hates her. And you can guess the next step: if her sins are bad enough, God might permanently withdraw his love.

This kind of thinking fuels Christian perfectionism, which forces a person to attempt to live a sin-free life. Since sin-free living is impossible, Christians like Diane soon see God as constantly angry at them.

When I was an undergraduate at the University of Texas, I was convinced of the very same lie. God was an off-again, on-again God, according to how I performed. I never felt secure in his love, since hardly a day went by I didn't sin in some form. God rarely seemed close or real. Soon, my own brand of Christian perfectionism burned me out, and I backed away from formal Christianity— church, Bible study, prayer—to regain some emotional balance. When you're on a perfection treadmill and you keep falling off, the only escape seems to be giving up altogether.

Then, about a year later, I came into contact with a student named Mike Ireland, who was the leader of Inter-Varsity Christian Fellowship at UT. Through Mike and other members of InterVarsity, a light bulb finally blinked on in my brain: God's love is unchanging. He wants me to live a godly life, but whatever I do, it doesn't affect how much he loves me. For the first time, I actually saw that God's love was always there. Always.

Where, traditionally, does the Earned Love lie come from? Diane had a clue. Since our parents are human, they express their love in conditional ways to one degree or another. Some of us coped with this by being "pleasers," giving Mom and Dad whatever it took to get their love. Others of us coped by being rebels, fighting our parents' demands. Some of us coped by being both. Then as we grew up and started to understand the concept called "God," we transferred our feelings toward our parents onto God as if he were just like them. It follows, then, that we would respond to God as we did to our parents by being a "pleaser," a "rebel," or both.

As adults, some of us grow into a more mature concept of God; others of us stay stuck in the old view, and the lie that God's love must be earned festers.

Can God's love be earned?

Absolutely not.

Do many Christians feel and act as if it has to be earned?

Absolutely!

The primary challenge to the Christian battling this lie is to confront it, not with feelings, but with what Scripture says about the issue. Believers in Ephesus were obviously living this lie when Paul wrote them, "For by grace you have been saved through faith, and that not of yourselves; it is the gift of God, not of works, lest anyone should boast."[2] He wrote Timothy that God called us to a holy life—not because of anything we have done but because of "His own purpose and grace."[3] And if we think God turns his back on us when we sin, we only have to look at Paul's words to the Romans about God's love: "God demonstrates His own love toward us, in that while we were still sinners, Christ died for us."[4]

Meditating on such statements so contradictory to our God's Love Must Be Earned lie is the first step toward acknowledging its falseness.

"God Hates the Sin and Sinner"

"Not only does God hate my sin, but he hates me when I sin. Furthermore, I should also hate myself."

When we buy into this misconception, we make turning away from the sin more difficult. Why? Because the energy it takes to turn from sin is used up by the self-hate we waste on ourselves. It mixes the Emotional Reasoning lie from the Distortion chapter with a misunderstanding of God's true concept of confession and forgiveness. The worst part, though, is that it is totally self-defeating, a vicious circle.

Jill struggled with this lie. She is a married mother of three and has been a Christian for a long time. She and her husband dated for several years before marrying. During the first few months they dated, she became pregnant with his child. She felt extremely torn about what to do. Her Christian values and beliefs told her to keep the baby and marry Dan. Yet neither of them wanted to get married at the time.

Jill, with Dan's urging, decided to have an abortion. Having an abortion so violated her Christian values, though, she became depressed. And she remained that way—for months, then years. She and Dan did finally get married and began having children. But Jill came to hate herself. She could not shake the guilt from her abortion and was convinced that God could never forgive her or love her again.

During our sessions, I found it painful to watch her. She had buried so many painful feelings, and she suffered so much self-hate.

"I can't seem to let go of what I did," she said on more than one occasion.

"You feel you don't deserve to let go of it and get on with life—is that right?"

She nodded, a crumpled Kleenex in her hand. "I don't deserve to be let off the hook for it."

"So," I answered, "you keep punishing yourself with depression and guilt."

"Surely God wouldn't want me to act like nothing happened!" she exclaimed.

"Would it surprise you if I said, that's exactly what he does want?"

"Yes, it would!" she shot back. "I can't believe that God wants me to forget this."

I stopped for a moment, letting her think about it. Then I said, "Do you really think that putting a wasted life on top of an aborted life is right?"

"What? What do you mean?"

"Do you believe in a God who wants you to throw your life away because of a wrong act you committed as a young woman?" I replied.

"Well, no," she began, "but it seems too easy to say it's over and I need to move on.

"Look," she said, almost impatiently, "somebody has to pay for what happened, and that's *me*."

"You've already paid for what happened. You confessed doing it. You haven't done it again. You've been depressed ever since you had the abortion. Adding more misery on top of it won't erase the past or please God."

She shook her head, her jaw jutting out. "My gut says you're wrong."

I considered her situation for a moment. She almost acted as if, in a warped way, she enjoyed her own form of penance. I tried another tack: "Can you see you're hating yourself not because God wants you to, but because it's your own way of making amends?"

No answer. She stared past me.

"Jill, you are taking what you think needs to be done and assuming that it's what God thinks too. Instead, God wants you to go on with your life."

She turned her head toward me, with the same blank look on her face. "It's too easy. If I can't forgive myself, how can God?"

Jill wouldn't let go. She chose the sackcloth and

ashes route, and I'm sad to say she's still berating herself. That is how stuck some of us get in the lie that hating ourselves is the only proper way to show sorrow for sin.

Diane, our average churchgoer from the beginning of the chapter, chose another route. She turned things around. On the day she took up that pen and pad and began to study what God says about the sin versus the sinner, willing to look at her life and beliefs differently from the way she'd been taught, she finally was on her way to grasping the concept of grace. It became a major theme in her life as she studied it, lived it, and moved away from the lie that both the sin and the sinner should be hated.

These women, Jill and Diane, are perfect pictures of the harm that can be done in the name of religion *and* the change in attitude fundamental to getting rid of lies and the future hurt they cause.

The biblical story of the woman caught in adultery is a wonderful example of God's true concept of the sin versus sinner relationship. You'll recall that several legalists of the time were acting as "religious cops" for God, rounding up Mosaic lawbreakers. They grabbed the adulterous woman and dragged her before Christ, whom they probably saw as some kind of moral sheriff.

According to Mosaic law, the woman should have been stoned to death right then. Knowing this, the teachers and Pharisees asked Christ what should be done—a trick question if there ever was one. His reaction: "He who is without sin among you, let him throw a stone at her first."[5] Of course, no one dared move, though I would guess a few of the Pharisees wanted to. What was Christ's point? All people sin, and we don't help sinners by beating them up or putting them to death. When he spoke to the woman, he captured God's attitude succinctly: "Neither do I condemn you; go and sin no more."[6]

Sin is usually its own punishment in terms of the natural consequences it brings. To heap on top of it our own personal penalty of self-hate seems absurd and is definitely unbiblical, even though many "religious" people would say the attitude is quite Christian. Yet, as one of my colleagues put it, that's like treating a sprained ankle by pounding it with a crowbar.

So what will it be? Jill's reaction? Or Diane's? The Pharisees' or Christ's? If you think you are letting yourself off the hook too easily by choosing to just hate sin and not yourself, let me suggest to you that just correcting your sin, even with God's help, will take every bit of effort you have. It is no easy approach.

You are really making a choice between your own human style of dealing with sin and the style God has laid out for us: correcting the sin, then correcting the damage we have done to others who've been affected by it, and finally dedicating ourselves to turning away from that sin in the future. Decide to do it God's way. It is the only way that promotes growth.

"Because I'm a Christian, God Will Protect Me from Pain and Suffering"

Jerry was one of those "success" Christians—he enjoyed showing his success and giving God the glory for his financial situation. That was the story until he lost that good job and found himself unemployed for six months. When he came to me, his overriding question, session after session, was, "Why did God let this happen? I thought he loved me."

"You seem to be assuming a loving God won't let bad things happen to you," I said.

He looked at me with a funny expression on his face. "Well, yes. If he lets bad things happen, how can he be loving?"

"What do you think?"

He didn't have a quick answer. Finally Jerry said, "Could be he's getting back for some sin in my life."

I waited. "Isn't that the old 'God messes up our lives to punish us for our sins' lie we've discussed before?"

"You're right. I suppose that's not it. But what else could it be?" Jerry looked genuinely puzzled. "He's never done this to me before."

Being a Christian means joy, peace, and contentment, we are told. We happily misconstrue that to mean a Christian never has problems or pain. We'll be protected by our all-powerful Bodyguard from losing our jobs, suffering from illness, or having accidents that happen to "other" people. We want to believe it, so we do. This one lie may be the most insidious religious falsehood in Christendom. Daily, hourly, people are hurt by it.

I've seen so many believers like Jerry whose "faith" becomes a source of bitterness and anger the moment life turns sour. God often becomes the scapegoat for all the hurt we feel when he doesn't come charging to the rescue like a heavenly cavalry, or more to the point, like the loving "Father Knows Best" father who always makes things right. "Isn't that love?" we ask childishly.

How then to explain the truth? The truth, as we've discussed earlier, is that life is difficult. Faith makes it less difficult, not by solving the problems through rescue, but by giving us a resource to handle the problems.

Free will is the hub, I believe, of our daily living and hurting. At the risk of oversimplifying, I believe God has given us free will and will not typically get in the way of our using it. He will allow us to make unhealthy choices that bring painful consequences. God will allow me, for instance, to drive my car a hundred miles an hour; and he won't necessarily step in and prevent me from killing myself.

And not only do we have free will, but everyone else has it as well. The unhealthy ways other people use their free will, then, can make our lives painful. For instance, Jerry, through no fault of his own, lost a job he loved. For us to have the gift of free will, God normally will not step in and stop such things from happening.

Don't Christians deserve it a bit easier, though, since we are Christians? What we deserve or don't deserve is not the issue. Anyone coming to Christianity for an easy ride through life has missed the point altogether.

In fact, as we discussed in chapter 2, when you examine closely what Christianity calls for—when you look closely at the most dedicated Christians of history—you can build a fairly solid case that being a Christian makes life *more* painful, not less. It's a lifestyle that requires "dying to self." It's a lifestyle of sacrifice, service, humility—actions and attitudes extremely difficult for any human being in our "do your own thing" and "you're #1" modern culture.

So how best to handle this lie? Jerry and I talked about this from a biblical point of view.

"Jerry, you've read the Book of James in the Bible, haven't you?"

"Sure," he said, matter of factly. "But I just can't believe I'm supposed to jump up and down for joy when I have problems. Maybe it's not translated right or something."

"C'mon, Jerry, what do you really think it is saying?"

"Okay, I know there's got to be some truth there," he said, making a resigned face. "I mean, maybe we're supposed to learn something from suffering, but I don't like it. My head tells me it's just not fair. I don't see what I can learn from losing my job. I mean how does being out of work teach me anything? I'm sure not going to 'count it all joy' that I'm suffering. All I'm learning is how much I miss my job."

"You're telling me you don't think you can learn anything from all this?" I asked, "You're saying that you can't learn something about yourself and God?"

Jerry looked caught. He knew the truth all right, but he didn't want to admit it. He just wanted his easy life back. His answer was a wry look that spoke volumes and gave us an opening to keep working on his healing.

We cannot learn without pain, Aristotle once said, summing up the great truth that counters the "God Will Protect Me from Pain and Suffering" lie. If we demand that learning be pain-free, we will almost automatically steer clear of experiences that hurt, or we'll deny them like Jerry and learn relatively little.

I'm convinced we knew Aristotle's truth as children, but we lost the knowledge along the way to adulthood. Nicholas, a boy who lives down the block from me, is trying to learn to ride his bike. I've watched him in the last few weeks. He's fallen and fallen and fallen again. He scrapes a knee and skins an arm, and he gets his mother to put a Band-Aid on them. Then he marches right back out and tries again. Finally, one afternoon, he miraculously rode all the way down the street without falling off. Oh, he had paid for it with bruised knees and many tears, but his willingness to suffer and his drive to succeed got him what he was after. He'll enjoy biking for the rest of his life.

The same can be true for us. Life is the classroom; God is the teacher; skinned and bruised egos are the price for learning. If, like Nicholas, we are courageous enough to keep trying, nothing can stop us from learning to "ride" through life without too many mistakes. But, we have to keep trying no matter how much it hurts.

"All My Problems Are Caused by My Sins"

Ever since the days of Job, people have been hearing and believing that problems are caused by sins. Logic holds no sway with this lie, which is the "God messes up our lives to punish us for our sins" lie that Jerry was buying into. Harold was the victim of that same old lie.

"I know why I'm having such trouble," he said. "I'm being punished." Harold was a distinguished older man I'd been working with for only a short time, and he opened one of our sessions with this statement.

"Punished? For what?" I said.

"Well," he hedged, "I don't know for sure. But I'm sure it's something we can find out. It's the only thing that makes sense."

"Harold, you believe, then, that the only time people have problems is when they sin?"

"Yes, it makes sense."

"Then that means that bad things only happen to bad people. Good people never have any troubles."

"Well, no, that's not what I said. Good people seem to have trouble . . ." He thought about that for a second, then clicked his fingers, "But maybe they're not as good as they seem to be!"

"And bad people who get away with awful crimes, they're not really bad?"

"No, no, no. Look, I don't know. There's some explanation for that, I'm sure," he said, with a wave of his hand.

We humans like to explain things. We like to explain the universe to each other, to have some tiny grasp of the future. Everything must happen for a reason, we feel. If we just know that reason, we can control the future somehow. To believe we cause all our own problems is a very easy lie to believe. If it's true, then all we have to do to keep out of trouble is be good. The problem is we cannot always *be* good, and, when we believe this lie on top of that inevitability, we doom ourselves to a guilt-ridden life we wouldn't wish on anyone.

Of course, as always, this lie has a toehold in reality. If you are carrying on an affair with someone at the office, problems can result from that sin. Other people's sin can hurt you too. If your partner decides to funnel off your business profits into a Swiss checking account, you will suffer. But what about the problems resulting from no sin at all? For example, our friends' home was struck by lightning. It burnt a hole in their roof, "fried" some of their electrical wiring, and ruined some appliances. Yet even in a situation like this, some Christians would start to think, *I must have done something wrong because otherwise God would not let that lightning strike my house.* If God used lightning to get back at us for our sins, every house in America would have been torched long ago!

We can see the truth, once again, in the ministry of Christ. When he and his disciples saw a man blind from birth, Christ's disciples asked Christ in so many words, "Rabbi, who sinned? This man or his parents? Who caused his blindness?"

"Neither this man nor his parents sinned," said Jesus. "but [this happened so] that the works should be revealed in him."[7]

Sometimes God allows bad things to happen to good people because he wants to display his power. Sometimes he allows it, as we discussed earlier, to help us mature.

Sometimes, through free will, as the Valley Girls say, "Stuff happens." The only truth we can grasp is that God can bring good out of bad. That's the truth behind the passage, "in all things God works for the good of those who love him."[8]

The challenge we face is to examine honestly the root of a given problem. If the root is personal sin, then that sin does need to be dealt with before the problem can be solved.

If, on the other hand, a problem is the result of someone else's sin or no sin at all, then we need to let ourselves off the hook and solve the problem as best we can. The alternative is to spend our lives feeling guilty over something we didn't cause, all because of a lie.

"It Is My Christian Duty to Meet All the Needs of Others"

Robert, a pastor friend of mine, is a bright, articulate, kind, caring man who loves people a great deal. During his ministry, he has helped thousands. One day, he dropped by my office, ostensibly to say hello. What I soon found out was that he was clinically depressed. His eyes were hollow, his shoulders hunched. He looked ill. All the signs of burnout were there.

"Robert," I said, beckoning him to have a seat, "how's work going?"

"I didn't get much sleep last night. For that matter, I didn't sleep all week. My phone rang every night, in the middle of the night, and I ended up running over to some members' houses," he said, slumping onto my couch.

"The thing is, I don't have time during the day to

take a nap to catch up. We're still looking for an assistant pastor, and my youth director just left. I've felt like I should wear running shoes to work this whole last year," he said with a sigh.

Well, his sense of humor isn't totally gone, I thought.

He went on. "Today, though, I couldn't get out of bed. I just couldn't move. I didn't get up till noon. So I dropped in on you."

Robert was in trouble. In his efforts to please God, he was suffering from severe emotional burnout, which made it impossible for him to carry on his ministry. Do you see the paradox of what he did? He worked so hard to please God and everyone else that he couldn't carry on his ministry at all.

This lie could also be called the "Christians never say no" lie, and it's a tape we play and replay every day. A woman from our church called to ask me to call on a family in our neighborhood who had visited our church recently. The request was totally appropriate, but my head told me I did not have time to do it. Since I would have felt guilty saying no, though, I said yes. I'm embarrassed to say that the family's name and address sat on my desk for two months yelling, "Chris, you said you'd do this!" Guess what? It never got done. By failing to be honest and assertive about my own priorities and limitations, I said yes when I needed to say no—all because of that lying tape in my head that says a good Christian never says no.

Many of us forget that we can only do so much to meet the needs of others and that God would not call us to live a life of meeting others' needs in a way that burn us out in the process. We tend to forget that Christ said: "Come to me, all you who labor and are heavy laden, and I will give you rest. Take my yoke upon you and learn from me. . . . For my yoke is easy and my burden is light."⁹ In spite of those words, many of us turn Christianity into a heavy, burdensome lifestyle that nobody of sound mind would want to live.

I always think of the story of Mary and Martha when I hear this lie in my patients' lives. In her efforts to be the perfect hostess to Jesus, Martha flew all over the place preparing things for her important guests. Mary, on the other hand, sat quietly at Christ's feet, listening, enjoying his presence. Martha, as most of us would, began to gripe about Mary's failure to help. "Don't you care that my sister has left me to do the work by myself? Tell her to help me!" she fairly shouted at Jesus. She was angry not only at Mary but also at Jesus.

Remember Jesus' answer? "Martha, Martha, you are worried and troubled about many things. But one thing is needed, and Mary has chosen that good part, which will not be taken away from her."¹⁰

Christ means that the Marthas of the world (of whom I happen to be one) spend their time worrying about the quantity of things to be done. They are prime candidates for despair, anger, bitterness, and burnout. The Marys of the world, who stop to experience life's quality, are primed for peace and meaning. Simply put, we were not called to do it all, only our part.

"A Good Christian Doesn't Feel Angry, Anxious, or Depressed"

Imagine, if you will, that you are crossing a street and a car comes barreling out of nowhere, right at you. At that moment, you experience the physiological "fight or flight" reaction. Your body gets a surge of adrenalin, your pupils dilate, your breathing becomes shallow, your muscles tense, and you feel very anxious as you dive to get out of the way. At that moment, would you say that your faith in God is weak?

No way.

Now imagine again. Your best friend cheats you. Your child dies. Your house is burglarized. You lose your job. How do you feel? How *should* you feel? You automatically feel some of the same emotional reactions that come from a physical threat or when you experience certain psychologically threatening realities. Would you be surprised, though, if I told you that many of my Christian patients feel that such "negative" emotions as anger, anxiety, and depression are wrong and automatic signs that one's faith is not up to par?

The belief that we shouldn't feel what we feel often results in "stuffing." Stuffing is taking what you feel and repressing or suppressing it so that you don't feel it. The feelings don't really go away, though. They stay buried in the unconscious or subconscious ready to come out when we tire of the effort expended to keep them stuffed. Ultimately, when too many feelings get "stuffed," the result is a very messy "spewing" of the logjam of emotions—which usually happens at the most inopportune times. Playing your "A good Christian is never angry or depressed" tape long enough can blow up in your face.

Well-meaning Christian friends wear grooves in this particular tape with such comments as:

"God hasn't forgotten you. You shouldn't be depressed."

or

"It must be God's will, so everything will work out."

or

"If you trust in God, you can 'in everything give thanks.'"

Aren't these comments true? Of course, but God didn't just give us pleasurable feelings. He gave us the whole emotional range, from pleasure to pain. If he gave us so many ways to feel, why would he want us to only experience the positive ones?

Instead, why can't we tell ourselves and those who are hurting: "Go ahead! Allow yourself to hurt and feel depressed! Get it out of your system so you don't have to carry it around the rest of your life! Grieve through it and then move on."

I get quite a few "stuffers" in my office. They come to me because they have stuffed so long they are emotionally sick from it. Julie, small and blond, a nail-biter, was a perfect example. She sat on my couch and nervously nibbled away for the first few minutes of every visit.

"Julie," I would finally say, "tell me what's bothering you."

Usually, she told me small things, never much about the real reason she'd finally come to me—the loss of her mother. She'd felt depressed for the three years since her mother died. But during one of our sessions, she cut straight through her little anxieties to the heart of her problem. She acknowledged her acceptance of a lie: "I feel so guilty about being so depressed. I know it's wrong."

"There's nothing wrong with feeling sad about losing your mother," I countered.

"But for three years?! I just think there's got to be

something wrong with my faith. Else why couldn't I get over this?"

"Julie, it took you almost three years to realize it was your mother's death that was depressing you," I said, quietly. "Allowing yourself to grieve is healthy. Not allowing yourself to grieve has made you chronically depressed. Does your faith say not to grieve?"

"No." She crossed her hands in her lap and looked at me. "Are you saying that God expects me to feel like this?"

My answer was yes, with qualifications. First, if painful emotions are a sign of a weak faith, then how do we account for the times Christ expressed strong emotions? He wept when Lazarus died. As he prayed in the Garden of Gethsemane, he told his disciples, "My soul is overwhelmed with sorrow to the point of death."[11] He shouted and overthrew tables when he confronted the moneychangers in the temple. Pretty strong emotions, wouldn't you say?

Sometimes, though, anger, anxiety, and depression may very well indicate a lack of faith in God and who he is. That is the qualification I mentioned above. How can we tell the difference? Let me suggest three questions to ask yourself: How often do I feel sad (angry, anxious)? How intense is my feeling? And how long have I experienced that feeling? A month? A year? Five years?

Strong emotions that show up *frequently* should make us question what's going on. For example, some Christians are anxious all the time, regardless of the circumstances. Such chronic anxiety may reflect a lack of faith in the fact that God does control the universe and a lack of faith in his promise that he will never make us face a problem we cannot handle with his help.

Emotions that are overwhelmingly *intense* may also be a sign our faith needs tending. If I lose my job and become so intensely depressed that I cannot function, perhaps I do not strongly believe in God's ability to help me handle problems. Be careful about what I'm saying, though. Certain events, like the death of a loved one, can be overwhelmingly intense and incapacitate us temporarily. If, for example, my wife or kids were to die, I'd be overwhelmed with grief, and normal, healthy functioning would be difficult for a while.

Finally, strong, painful emotions that last a long time may signal a problem with faith. If we stay anxious, depressed, angry about an event for the next thirty years, maybe we don't have sufficient faith in God's ability to run the universe. I've counseled Christians who have stayed angry and depressed over certain events *all* their lives. Their faith is so weak they cannot forgive or forget—which God asks us to do in no uncertain terms.

While we need to give ourselves permission to feel what we feel, at the same time we must be honest enough to examine whether or not the feeling fits what has happened to us. Neither "stuffing" nor "spewing" what we feel usually helps. The middle ground is to accept what we feel and express it in ways that help us move on.

"God Can't Use Me Unless I'm Spiritually Strong"

Finally, a short explanation about a very widespread lie. As a college student, I remember playing this "favorite" tape over and over. I would want to tell friends about Christ, but I felt my life was such a mess that God couldn't work through me. I was convinced they'd look at my life and say, "Hey, you haven't done so well. Why should I listen to *you*?" Even today, I'd love to tell close friends about God, but I find myself playing that same old college tape in my head. How can I tell them about God if my life doesn't show shining proof of all I'm declaring?

Yet one of Christianity's paradoxes is that through our weaknesses God can show power. Our own arrogance is an underlying cause of this lie. We're assuming God can't do what he wants unless we are strong, when, frankly, he can do anything he wants through anybody he wants, anytime, and no one can stop him—except perhaps, if that "anybody" says no.

I also see this as an offshoot of that #1 Self-Lie, "I must be perfect." How can I glorify God until I lead the perfectly perfect life? we ask. The question then becomes, How does anything get done, since only one person has ever led the perfect life?

Paul is a good example of the falseness of this lie. In a letter to the Corinthians, Paul even admits to delighting in his weaknesses: "For when I am weak, then I am strong."[12]

I've realized I don't have to be a spiritual giant to tell people about God. In fact, my being honest about my own weaknesses and struggles gives those I tell a healthier, more realistic picture of Christianity—one, I hope, devoid of lies. As Christ said, it's not the healthy who need a doctor, but the sick.[13]

The bottom line is that we are all "sick" and in need of the Doctor. We are always going to be less than perfect representatives of Christianity when we talk with others, no matter what level of Christian maturity we ultimately attain. Pretenses otherwise are hurtful and unhealthy. What better favor can we do potential Christians than to allow them to see the reality of the Christian struggle so they won't have to be stuck with playing taped lies through their own heads.

One last word. For those of us who believe some or all of the lies we've discussed, one of the critical actions we must take to erase our tapes is to study the Bible more carefully and see what it *really* says. Hand-me-down interpretations are easily misconstrued. I've used Scriptures over and over in my explanations in this chapter; and when I spot a religious lie in my practice, I do the same, because ultimately the truth—the correct understanding of the Scriptures—is the best way to break the religious lies so prevalent in Christianity today.

In fact, the How-To I've reserved for this chapter deals directly with this all-important point.

HOW TO DEFEAT YOUR LIES

First, I'd like to suggest an important How-To. It's called Thought Stopping. There are times for all of us when, no matter how much truthful self-talk we use, our lies and the emotional damage they wreak just won't go away. Thought Stopping is very useful in such situations. If you are the type that tends to be obsessed with issues or concerns, this will be effective in your thinking. First, focus on the very thought that produces anxiety (or anger or depression or guilt) for you. Then after 15 to 30 seconds, shout "Stop!" or make some loud noise. Perhaps you might set a timer. This action interrupts your thoughts and interrupts the emotions associated with them. After doing this a number of times, you might want to tone down your shout or just create some other diversion which will be your signal to stop.

For instance, you might be like Diane at the beginning of the chapter. You have caught yourself believing that you must earn God's love. You might even picture God as frowning, always sizing you up. Plan your noise that will stop your thinking, then focus on that image. When your shout or your alarm sounds, you might then focus on the true image you are learning to make your own.

Thought Stopping helps you by interrupting the thoughts that create emotional turmoil in your mind. It demonstrates that when irrational thoughts—lies—are eliminated (whether it be through disputing them with the truth or stopping the thought altogether), your emotional well-being does improve. Obviously, this approach doesn't, by itself, eliminate the lies that produce emotional problems, but it does help to stop them for a period of time and thus reduce your emotional wear and tear.

My second How-To is a very important one. For the Christian the most critical step in defeating lies, religious and otherwise, deals with two familiar but often misused practices: Scripture memorization and meditation.

Now, before you shrug off this idea, stop for a moment and read my statement again. The words *Scripture memorization and meditation* are too familiar, aren't they? We connect them with Sunday school or Bible study group or some organized church class, and we usually feel quite a bit of guilt about rarely doing either of the two at home. Viewing memorization and meditation as a serious and highly successful way to get rid of lies is a whole other idea, isn't it?

Take that idea seriously, though. Why? Because I've seen the amazing difference it can make in the lives of believers battling religious lies. I've also seen it work wonders with a Christian's other lies.

Interestingly enough, the Bible places tremendous emphasis on "mind renewal," and the biblical brand of mind renewal is accomplished through spending time memorizing and meditating on verses that directly teach the truth about our lies. (Appendix A is a list of Scripture verses I think are especially good ones for combating lies. They will give you an excellent start.)

In a very real sense, the Bible is God's primary way of giving us the most important truths we need to fight our lies. It's no coincidence that Satan was called the "father of lies."[14] Picture your situation this way: God and Satan are locked in this tremendous struggle for control of your mind. God's weapon is the truth, of course. Satan's is lies. Each day is a battle. Will you play those lie tapes? Or will you listen to the truth? To the degree we choose truth, we'll react appropriately to what happens to us and experience a peace which transcends all understanding.[15] To the degree we choose lies, we will be emotionally and spiritually miserable. When it's a mixture, as it usually is, we live with mixed emotional and spiritual signals.

Okay, I hear you saying, but how do I go about doing all this memorizing and meditating? If you're like the rest of us, the only way to do it is to make both a part of your regular routine. You might start with a small goal like one verse a week, maybe even one verse a month. (Working on only one verse a month may sound like too little, but you'd be surprised how difficult even that amount is for most Christians. I've found it's better not to push yourself at first or you won't do it at all.) Then take that verse and run it and rerun it through your head *daily* until it becomes a part of your thinking. You reflect on that verse, spending time running it through the deepest levels of your mind and considering how to use it in your daily life.

For example, the verse "For all have sinned and fall short of the glory of God" is one that most Christians know and most have memorized.[16] What does it *mean*, though?

Let's meditate on it for a moment. Thinking about the fact that *all* have sinned might lead you to seeing more deeply how *all* people are alike: we all fall short of being like God.

Thinking on that idea, in turn, might make you consider how morally similar we are to each other and how morally unique God is.

Thinking on *that* idea just might lead you to feel less isolated from others. Those you've always felt were "better" than you don't seem that much different anymore. By the same token, those you've felt were perhaps a bit "worse" than you don't seem that much different either. The moment you begin to see other people in the same light as you see yourself, you'll notice that interpersonal relationships become easier.

Last, all this meditating just might give you a deeper respect for God. The moment that you begin to see God in that unique light, you very possibly will experience a more worshipful and submissive attitude toward the Creator of All.

That's quite a bit to get from that small, familiar verse—and notice that we considered all that in a very short amount of time. What if you gave yourself a week to ponder the verse?

Meditating on what a verse means and how it can apply to your life is the surest way I know to sink truth into the deepest levels of our minds, down where our lies operate. It allows God, through the work of the Holy Spirit, to penetrate the lies that most affect our views of ourselves, others, and the world.

Without exception, all great men and women of the faith are also great students of Scripture. They have head knowledge of the Bible, but they also have heart knowledge. When you have both, spiritual growth is sure to follow. To use what is taught in the Bible, to know not only what its verses say but what they mean, is an awesomely powerful way to transform anyone's life. The power of God in this one effort alone gives us that significant edge we need to win the war against the "father of lies."

Don't just think about trying this How-To. Do it, even if it's only one verse a month. You'll be so excited about how it blows away the smokescreen covering so many of your lies that you won't stop for anything.

PART THREE

LIVING WITH TRUTH

7.

The Truth About Truth

Seek the truth,
Listen to the truth,
Teach the truth,
Love the truth,
Abide by the truth,
And defend the truth,
Unto death.

John Hus

"**Y**ou talk a lot about lies," all my patients say to me. They then ask the same question the young woman sitting in my office this morning asked. "What about truth?" she said. "I have a feeling there are some things you haven't told me."

She was right, of course. We had talked at length about the lies she was living, and she had done a good job of rejecting many of them, but she'd begun to notice that the result was not instant happiness and success. She then came upon an important insight: knowing and fighting the lies in our lives is one thing; taking the leap toward spiritual and mental health by filling those lie-sized holes with truth is another.

As you continue to fight your lies and move toward a life based on truth, there are certain realities about truth you should know—the truth about the truth.

Put yourself in the place of my "truth-seeking" patient, and let's first explore the truth about truth.

"Where do you want to start?" I asked her.

"I take it you're telling me there's a lot to talk about," she said, cocking an eyebrow. "I was afraid of that."

"There's good and there's bad. But knowing it all will help you. Of that, I am sure."

She sat up straight. "Okay, then. I want to hear it all."

"Tell me what is bugging you the most right now about working toward truth, and we'll start there," I suggested.

THE TRUTH COMES PIECE BY PIECE

"I'll tell you what's bugging me. Why does the truth sometimes seem so hazy? Why can't I see it all at once?" my patient asked.

I began explaining to her that truth, generally speaking, is not something we receive all at once in a life-changing, road to Damascus manner. Anaïs Nin said that there are very few human beings who receive truth, complete and staggering, by instant illumination. Most of them, she said, "acquire it fragment by fragment on a small scale . . . like a laborious mosaic."

That's a good mental image. I see truth more like putting together a thousand-piece puzzle. Piece by piece, we look for truth and attempt to "fit" it together. The effort to see what fits and what doesn't is painstaking. Our lies, the false pieces that don't fit in, didn't get there overnight, nor will they leave overnight. So we have to be patient with the process of exchanging our lies for the truth.

"I never could finish one of those puzzles," she muttered. "What else?"

There's another painful truth about truth, I told her. With our truth puzzle, we don't have all thousand pieces to work with and we won't before our time for putting the puzzle together is over. Simply put, we just don't know the whole truth while we live.

"Well, then who does?" asked my truth-seeking patient, a bit peeved.

Of course, that is *the* question, isn't it? And one we are intended to ask. As Carl Jung, one of the leaders of modern psychology put it, "Are we related to something infinite or not? That is the telling question of life."

Almost everyone wonders whether or not something infinite exists. Highly intelligent people have argued all positions on this issue, some concluding that there is no infinite being, some concluding that there is (giving us an amazing array to choose from), and some deciding that we can't know so we shouldn't worry about it. I agree with Jung, though. Whether or not there is an infinite being and whether or not we are related to it is life's most telling question. If "it" does exist, then we must ask, "What is 'it' like?" and "What does 'it' want?"

Hundreds of books have addressed this question, and the answer is beyond the scope of this one. But I am convinced that we have to address Jung's question in our personal lives before we can move on to deeper levels of understanding and recognizing truth. My own answer to Jung's question is "Yes!" and that the "something infinite" is the Creator—God—and he alone knows the whole truth. As Montaigne put it, "We are born to inquire into the truth; it belongs to a greater power to possess it." He will make the important pieces of the puzzle, those which keep our lives connected and whole, available to us if we seek the truth through him. And that is what I attempt to lead my patients to do—to seek out the truth available to them and to live by it.

"Okay, okay," my patient interrupted. "But you've never come out and said what truth *is* or how I find it and know it."

Put succinctly, we can know we have found truth when we see reality without frills, unvarnished. To get to this unvarnished reality, we must rely on God as the ultimate source of truth in our lives. We can't rely on what feels true, what someone we trust tells us is true, or what our favorite speaker or author says is true. These reliances leave the door open for our own pathology—as we psychologists call it—our own self-centeredness, ignorance, defensiveness to enter in and turn lies into destructive "truths." Rather, we must rely on God's help as we seek to discern the truth.

While we can know many important pieces of life's puzzle through knowledge, fact, logic, and experience, the most critical pieces—those that go beyond these sources—must be revealed by God and accepted by us on faith. The pieces available through both experience and divine disclosure are sufficient for knowing God, knowing what he wants from us, and knowing how to live emotionally healthy and meaningful lives. Theologian Thomas Aquinas put it like this: "Human salvation demands the divine disclosure of truths that surpass reason."

If we accept the Bible as God's Word, we have a guide. We can learn why and how to explore the Bible for truth:

> All Scripture is given by inspiration of God, and is profitable for doctrine, for reproof, for correction, for instruction in righteousness, that the man of God may be complete, thoroughly equipped for every good work.[1]

Of course, it's been far too easy in recent years to be confused about exactly how the believer should interpret the Bible. And as we've seen in the religious lies chapter, those around us can use the Bible itself to teach us lies. That fact, though, is not a reason to discontinue using the Bible as a guide to understanding the truth from God's viewpoint. It only means we should proceed carefully, eyes and minds open. Then the truths of the Bible will become the measure of other "truths." The Bible is the most direct way to seek God's truth.

Seeking truth, though, also means seeking God in every corner of life. The more we know of the mind of God through intense Bible study with an open, inquisitive mind and the more we balance what we learn with knowledge, fact, and logic, the easier it is to make the best possible decisions.

TRUTH—A PREREQUISITE FOR HEALTH

"You're giving me a headache, Dr. Thurman," my truth-seeking patient said, rubbing her temples. "If truth is that hard to grasp, why does anybody attempt to know it?"

That's a very good question.

We must seek truth and live by what is true because what we see as truth is what primarily determines our path through life. Psychiatrist Scott Peck states this nicely:

For truth is reality. That which is false is unreal. The more clearly we see the reality of the world, the better equipped we are to deal with the world. The less clearly we see the reality of the world—the more our minds are befuddled by falsehood, misperceptions, and illusions— the less able we will be to determine correct courses of action and make wise decisions. Our view of reality is like a map. . . . If the map is true and accurate, we will generally know where we are, and if we have decided where we want to go, we will generally know how to get there. If the map is false and inaccurate, we generally will be lost.[2]

There is another important reason why we must seek the truth and live by it. There is a direct, inescapable connection between our self-esteem and whether or not we are dedicated to truth. If dedication to truth characterizes our way of living, we develop stable positive feelings of worth. The moment we wrap our lives around lies, genuine feelings of self-worth are virtually impossible. We've all had moments in our lives when we suddenly saw that something we believed to be true was false. Instantly, the truth cuts like a knife. The writer of Proverbs wrote that as a man "thinks in his heart, so is he."[3]

BARRIERS TO KNOWING THE TRUTH

"Yeah," my truth-seeking patient said in response, "but it still sounds as if we can miss the truth altogether, even if we know all this stuff. There seem to be quite a lot of barriers to knowing truth."

She was exactly right. Among the many barriers to knowing the truth are prejudice and pride. Prejudice is a barrier to knowing the truth because your mind is already made up. Pride is a significant barrier to knowing the truth because it makes us arrogantly believe we already know the truth whether we do or not. With prejudice and pride, the truth can come right up and bite us on the nose and still go unnoticed.

Jeff was like that. He thought that his mother was a saint. He never questioned her in his whole life—which was more than thirty years. After he was married, he still catered to her every wish and looked upon her opinion as etched in stone. As you might imagine, his wife was not thrilled when she realized how deep this prejudice about his Mom went. As you also might imagine, their marriage was sinking fast. Before it went down for the last time, though, he came for counseling—only to please his wife.

"Actually, I think this is silly," he said to me after several sessions. "My wife is just jealous of my mother.

There isn't a woman like my mother in the world. The woman is wiser than anyone I've ever known."

"What makes you think that?" I asked. He looked at me as if I'd committed blasphemy.

"She sacrificed everything for me to have a good education, a head start in the world. She brought me and my brother up all by herself after my father ran off."

"Does your brother feel the way you do?" I asked.

"No, and I've never forgiven him for that. He goes on and on about her being domineering. Imagine that! Mother domineering!"

Jeff continued to see me for several weeks, until abruptly he quit. His wife told me he couldn't stand the fact that I questioned his mother's virtues. The last I heard, his wife was seriously contemplating divorce. Jeff had made up his mind, and nothing was going to change it, especially not the truth. Jeff's prejudice about his Mom's saintliness kept him from seeing the truth about how enmeshed they were. His marriage paid the price. Pride also got in his way of knowing the truth. He had a burning desire to look as if he knew the truth when he didn't.

As a college professor, I sometimes felt compelled to answer students' questions even when I had no earthly idea what I was talking about. That went on until one day a student asked me a question I knew I could not answer. Instead of bluffing my way through just to keep my professorial dignity intact, I looked straight at him and told him I wanted him to find that answer himself and report back to me. I still couldn't say I didn't know the answer, but I finally understood what was going on. Looking good was more important to me than knowing the truth. For a long time that need continued to be all-important; and while it did, I found it very easy not to pursue the truth. My pride was in the way.

So while there are many barriers to knowing the

truth, prejudice and pride are two of the worst. We must want truth and the health it brings more than anything, or our minds will play tricks, our pathology warping what we see. I tell my patients every day, though, that if they will commit to truth, no matter what happens, they will be rewarded with emotional and spiritual health.

TRUTH OFTEN LEADS TO PAIN

"Hmmm," my truth-seeking patient replied. "I can see that. I can also see that all this effort is not altogether pleasant, either, is it?"

My answer was the old adage, "The truth hurts." Then I reminded her of the hundreds of ways we use lies to escape pain of one kind or another. Speeders sometimes lie to police officers in order to avoid the pain of a traffic ticket. Students sometimes lie to teachers to avoid the pain of turning in a term paper on time. (When I was a university professor, one of my students had four grandfathers die in one semester!) Some taxpayers lie on their tax returns in order to avoid the pain of paying extra money to the government. You could add your own to the list, I'm sure.

Truth is painful. Most of us don't like to hear the real truth about ourselves and will sometimes react with hurt, even anger, when we do. Also truth is sometimes painful because it forces us to give up lies that we may have grown accustomed to and/or ones with which we feel secure. Giving up what makes us feel secure—even if it's miserable security—is hard.

Remember the story of Frank Serpico, the New York City policeman who was one of those rare men—an honest one. When he saw all the graft and illegal acts his fellow policemen were committing, he had to make a very painful decision, whether or not to tell the truth. He knew the high price he would pay either way. If he failed to tell the truth about police corruption, he would become part of the corruption himself. If he told the truth, he would be ostracized and scorned by his fellow officers, maybe even murdered. Yet, he told the truth. The ending is not altogether a happy one. His willingness to tell the truth helped clean up the New York City police force, but his personal and professional life suffered heavily. He received death threats for years, his health faltered, and he finally left the police force and the city. Telling the truth was extremely painful for him and for us as well.

"Hmmmph," my truth-seeking patient grunted at my illustration. "Maybe you better tell me again why commitment to truth is so important for me."

It's easy to feel that way. Now you know why so many people live with lies. Very few of us will be put to so strenuous a test as Frank Serpico, but the truth about ourselves and our personal lives can potentially be packed with pain and upheaval before it leads us to emotional health. We need resolve and awareness to get through the pain to the truth.

KNOWING TRUTH MAY MEAN BEING WILL-ING TO DOUBT

"I tell you what is hard, though," my truth-seeking patient said, gazing past me. "I find it really hard to go back on some of the things I was taught as a child. It's really hard to doubt some of those things, even when the adult part of me is saying I should. Is this bad or good?" she asked me.

Doubting is often a must, I answered her. We need to doubt many of our beliefs in order to know if they are true. If you believe that doubt is evil, especially doubt of theological teachings, this truth may be hard to digest. I think, though, that doubt is a God-given ability that helps us to take what we hear and test its truth. In fact, I think

God wants us to doubt what we hear, even from a minister's mouth, so that we know *why* we believe what we believe.

Lloyd, a young man in his early twenties, was seeing me because his anxiety made him unable to function in his personal life. Lloyd grew up in a fundamental church. Many of the beliefs they taught him as a child he never questioned, but took them as unalterable truth and carried them into adulthood. Adult life, though, had recently been butting against some of these traditions.

One of those teachings was that only those who went to his specific church were actually true believers. You see, Lloyd had done the unthinkable. He'd fallen in love with a woman of another denomination. She professed Christianity and in many ways was more devout than Lloyd, but Lloyd was having tremendous anxiety over their upcoming marriage. He could not let go of those early strict teachings, which is exactly what I had just suggested in our session.

"What do you mean?!" Lloyd shot back. "Everybody I grew up with believes the way I do. I learned that as a child. You're asking me to doubt?"

"Lloyd," I asked, "do you believe that your fiancée is not a believer?"

"Of course not. She's a wonderful Christian," he said, stiffening.

"Then why is it hard to throw off this strict childhood belief?" I asked knowing the answer. "Why can't you doubt some of those things you were taught?"

He gave me a pained expression. "Well, I've always believed that doubting is sin."

I leaned back in my chair. "Lloyd, I really understand—for a very good reason," I said. "You see, I was raised in the same church and told the same kind of lie. I know how hard it is to doubt something you were told by people you trusted, especially when it has a 'God sugarcoat' over the top of it."

"You, too?" he said, his eyes wide. "Then you're saying it's okay to doubt?"

"Lloyd," I said, "it's not only okay to doubt, but I believe it's often fundamental in order to grasp the truth. You can't have secondhand beliefs and be emotionally healthy. Constructive doubt can help you solidify your own beliefs."

It's hard to buck a crowd, though, isn't it? Longstanding customs can be hard to doubt. The basic message we hear is: "But we never did it that way before. This can't be right. We've always thought *this* way."

Does this attitude remind you of an incident in the Bible? I always think of the crowd who chose Barabbas over Christ. What would you have done if you had been in that crowd? We can let popular opinion sway us, receive approval when we go along with it, yet be following a lie. It takes an honest and courageous person to step out of the crowd and say, "I don't care how the rest of you think; I'm going to stand by what I think is true!"

What's the alternative? Blindly accepting a secondhand belief system from our parents, ministers, teachers, and friends who are just as susceptible to lies as we are.

Remember Thomas, the doubting disciple? I'm a Thomas, and like people from Missouri, I want you to show me before I can believe. There's an important exception to this "show me" attitude, though. If you've ever looked closely at Thomas's encounter with the resurrected Jesus Christ, you'll notice that once Christ gave Thomas the evidence he wanted, Christ demanded that Thomas believe.[4] Doubt is good, to a point. Anyone, though, who needs repeated proof of the same truth may never make a commitment to it at all.

AN UNEXCITING TRUTH CAN BE ECLIPSED BY A THRILLING LIE

My truth-seeking patient nodded as I made the above points. "I can certainly see that not doubting would be a problem," she said. "But what I have the most trouble with is the lies that sound *so-o-o-o* good."

She was right. Many of the lies we won't doubt are the ones we want to be true. Some lies just sound better than the truth.

Isuzu ran a series of funny TV commercials. In them, a salesman with a pasted-on smile and a very slick look spent the whole commercial lying to us about what the car offers us—twin satellite dishes, a frozen yogurt machine, six hundred miles per gallon of gas, and many more outlandish options. The commercials were popular because we knew he was lying and could laugh at his outlandish selling style. Unfortunately, the people who lie to us in life aren't so obvious and mix in just enough truth to make what they say sound true, and if we like what we hear, we are tempted to swallow the lie whole.

What are some of these lies? We've discussed many of them in the Worldly Lies chapter. The You Can Have It All lie may be the worst offender. We want to believe it. Who among us doesn't want it all? So we listen, hear a *bit* of truth (that you can have some of it), and then believe it all.

In the Religious Lies category, one flagrant lie that hurts many people today is the health and wealth gospel based on the Have It All lie. It thrills us to think that God is just as interested in our financial prosperity as he is our spiritual prosperity. If we are not blessed with wealth, though, we worry that somehow we are not "making the grade." We ignore the truth that most of our spiritual giants have been financially impoverished.

Thrilling lies can be seen every day in advertising. Unthrilling products have to be sold, so they are labeled "amazing!" or "breakthrough," or "new, new new!" when in reality they aren't any of the above. Mouthwash that claimed to stop colds was a thrilling idea but proved to be a lie. Others, such as toothpaste that offers sex appeal, we know to be silly, but we'll buy the products anyway because we like the idea. The worst examples of this sort of abuse are even criminal. You may have read about the baby food scandal in which a well-known and trusted baby food company actually sold colored water as apple juice. We were told that the executives that made the decision to lie to the consumer were decent family men themselves—but obviously ones who were so caught up in their own lies that they could lie to the public and feed babies colored water.

Of course, thrilling lies aren't exclusively a product of religion or advertising. We hear them daily from our next door neighbors and coworkers and ourselves. As barriers to truth go, the thrilling lie is a big one, especially when it is mixed with a bit of truth.

THE TRUTH WILL STAND FOREVER

I need to point out something very important to my truth-seeking patient and to you. We need to believe that when all is said and done, the truth will remain. We must see the truth as something so inherently pure and strong that nothing, not even the end of life on earth, will cause it to fail. If we do not see the truth as eternal, our commitment to it will be weak and we will be unable to use it to grow and mature. German monk Johannes Eckhart said, "Truth is something so noble that if God could turn aside from it, I would keep to the truth and let God go." I agree with Eckhart. What kind of God would we have if he could turn away from truth? Fortunately, God will not do any such thing, so we obviously don't need to worry about letting him go. The truth has to be our bottom line. Along with English reformer John Wycliffe, we have to believe that "in the end the truth will conquer."

8.

The Truth About Change

My truth-seeking patient and I ended our conversation about truth. We both sat quietly a moment, lost in our thoughts. Then she drew a big breath and leaned back heavily on the sofa.

"Wow," she said, shaking her head. "You don't make it sound easy. But I guess you're right. Knowing all those truths about the truth will help."

She paused, checked her watch, then with one of her most earnest looks, she leaned toward me, elbows on her knees, and said, "I've got to admit, though, there's something I'm more worried about. I'm starting to fight my lies, and I don't know what I can expect. Do you know what I'm going to go through?"

Whenever any of us attempt to defeat our lies and replace them with the truth, there is a certain pattern that we will go through. I've seen this pattern hundreds of times in the lives of my patients as they struggled with their lies in an effort to get back to the truth. I've seen it in my own life. Odds are that you will go through this

177

pattern when you attempt to exchange your lies for the truth.

Let me describe this pattern for you so you can know what to expect.

PHASE ONE—LIVING IN PAIN

"So you want to know what to expect?" I asked her.

"Definitely. Forewarned is forearmed," she said. "I'm all ears."

"Okay. Let's take it step by step through your experience. I can actually give you four phases," I said, settling back in my chair. "In phase one, you believed certain lies that created a fairly stable level of misery for you, right?"

"That's the truth," she said, rolling her eyes.

"But just like most people, even though your lies created misery, you stayed with them. It's something psychologists refer to as the 'neurotic paradox' where you hang on to certain ways of acting or thinking even though they are self-destructive or painful."

"That's like the alcoholic who keeps drinking even though it's ruining his life or the overweight person who keeps eating too much even though it makes him unhappy," she added.

"Exactly," I said. "You knew you had a problem you needed to change, but you did nothing significant to change it."

"Don't remind me. What about phase two?" my truth-seeking patient prodded.

PHASE TWO—THE PAIN WORSENS

"In phase two, you made the big decision to do something about your problem and began to make some effort to change."

"Yeah, that's where I am, all right," she agreed.

"At the point of doing something about the problem, most likely you're going to feel worse."

"Great," she sighed.

"In other words, at the very point where you try to change your lies, emotional pain in your life increases. A good analogy is the overweight person you mentioned who decides to lose weight by exercising and dieting. The first few days or weeks are the worst. Not only is that person still overweight, but now he has sore muscles and feels worse. The emotional pain of being overweight and trying to do something about it is worse than the emotional pain of just being overweight."

"I know what comes next," my truth-seeking patient interrupted. "For some people that's too much, so they bail out—go back to phase one as the lesser of two evils, right?"

"Exactly," I agreed. "In fact, bailout is a problem anytime, but phase two is the most tempting time."

"What's going to get me through phase two then?" she asks.

"Well, most people's ability to get through phase two is partially, if not largely, tied to their ability to delay gratification. If you have to have immediate payoffs for your hard work, you'll rarely complete phase two. But if you're willing to work diligently over a long period of time before you receive your 'reward,' you'll make it."

She groaned, flipping a hand in frustration. "I'm gonna have a miserable time," she confessed.

"It's that way for everybody," I consoled her. "Phase two is so difficult that we all need tremendous support and encouragement to get through it."

PHASE THREE—FROM PAIN TO PLEASURE

"All right, you've given me the bad news," my truth-seeking patient said. "Surely phase three is better?"

"Well, in phase three you'll begin to see some of the positive results of your hard work, and your pain level will start to decline. But the early stages of phase three still have a lot of the pain from phase two, and you'll be working hard just to get back to the level of pain you experienced in phase one."

"Back to misery?!" she exclaimed.

I smiled. "Really, this is an important point because bailout is still a possibility in phase three. So you have to be aware of it. But the best part . . ."

"Oh good, there *is* a best part!" she said.

"The best part is that your hard work will show more and more positive results, and you'll begin to feel hope and encouragement."

She sat up, almost smiling. "Go on!"

"And those feelings will start to dominate phase three. Optimism and hope become stronger and stronger until you break even and feel yourself going farther and farther, better and better."

"Go on! Go on!" she persisted.

"Then there's phase four," I said.

PHASE FOUR—THE PLATEAU

"Surely phase four is good," she said, expectantly.

"It's a leveling off. The hard work of phases two and three will bloom, and you'll probably feel tremendous accomplishment."

"Good," she said, grinning.

"There's a danger, though," I began.

"I kinda thought there would be."

"The danger," I explained, "is that you may bask in the joy and satisfaction of your accomplishment and lose sight of the fact that you must continue the hard work that brought you to phase four, or it will all be washed away."

"So even when I finally have my act together, I can't let up?" she asked.

"Right," I answered. "See, phase four involves pain too—contrary to the myth that you can reach a point of *nirvana* when pain goes away—because you still have to work to maintain the success you've achieved. For a dieter, losing weight doesn't mean he won't have to work to keep it off."

"But surely I've learned enough along the way to help me stay in phase four," she said.

"That's right. It's one of the nice things about phase four. The work habits you develop during phases two and three usually help you maintain all those positive results you have plugged into your life. You take all your knowledge and all your experience, and you use them to keep those old habits and lies away from you."

"I guess it all depends on how deeply embedded and dangerous the lie you're getting rid of is," she thought out loud.

"Definitely. The depth of pain in phase two, for instance, differs quite a bit from person to person and from problem to problem," I explained. "Your problems, for instance, are deeply ingrained but not as much as, say, those of an adult who was molested as a child. But smaller problems . . ."

"Like not admitting mistakes or expecting life to go my way?" she asked.

"Yes, those problems won't be as painful to face and therefore will be easier to improve. And, of course, how long a person stays in each phase also depends on the person's work habits and determination.

"Speaking as a lazy person, just exactly what do you mean?" she said, frowning.

"Well, I mean that some people might actually stay in phase one their whole lives because of weak and passive work habits, while others zip through the four phases quickly because they work more assertively."

"How far can I go in phase four?" she asked.

"You may level off in phase four at a different place

from somebody else because a person's gifts and abilities tend to set the limit—the 'success ceiling.' In other words, there will always be someone better than you and someone worse than you in a given area of life. But all you've got to worry about is cleaning up your own backyard."

My truth-seeking patient grew very quiet. She squirmed a little, then drummed her fingers on the armrest. "Dr. Thurman, is there no easier way to do all this?"

"Remember when you tried that 'quit smoking' plan? What was it? 'Quit smoking in three minutes,'" I asked.

"Yeah, don't remind me. It should have read, 'Quit smoking *for* three minutes," she griped.

"Hey, the world knows that we're all suckers for this kind of sales pitch because we want to improve without going through any pain," I said. "It's the 'Great Myth' about change—that it can be done painlessly. Does that answer your question?"

"Okay, let's get specific here, just so I know I've got this straight," she said. "You know I've got a problem with the lie that I have to be perfect."

"Right, and your phase one, when you weren't doing anything to change it, was awful, wasn't it?"

"Definitely, or I'd never have come to see you," she said.

"In phases two and three you've gone through the pain and hard work of realizing that you aren't God, to err is human, that life is difficult, and that with God's help you do the best you can. And as those truths start to take over your mind, there is much less emotional suffering, and so more energy is left over to live life more fully. This energy will take you right up to the higher levels of success in phase four. You couldn't ever have reached phase four by using perfectionism."

"And for the future?" she asked.

"The answer to whether or not you stay in phase four will be tied to whether or not you stay dedicated to the truth or revert back to the lie."

"It's certainly all up to me, isn't it?" she said, in more of a statement than a question.

"It certainly is."

AN EXAMPLE

My truth-seeking patient sighed. "Could we try an example from my own experience?"

"Okay," I said. "Let's take a small thing, one you've already worked through."

"Fine," she said. "Small things tend to become big things for me, as you know. I bet I know which small thing you're going to use, too."

"Remember when we had that misunderstanding about whether or not I would see your daughter in therapy?"

"Yes. That would be a good one."

"Now, granted, the misunderstanding was my fault. I told you I would see her . . ." I began.

"And then when I called to make the appointment, your secretary said you weren't taking any new patients," she finished.

"Which I had told my secretary to tell people."

"It was still a week until our own session, so I had a whole week to stew on it. At first, I got so upset about it."

"But instead, what did you do?" I asked.

"I brought my journal entry with me to our session," she said.

"I've still got it too. Let me get it out. Using the ABCDE approach you learned to defeat the lies you told yourself, you sat down and recorded the event that had occurred, the lies that had upset you, and your emotional response to them. Then, you countered those lies with the truth," I said. I dug for the paper. "Ah, here it is."

My truth-seeking patient's journal entry looked something like this:

A—THE EVENT: Dr. Thurman told me he would meet with my daughter, but his secretary said he was not taking any new patients.

B—SELF-TALK: This isn't fair. Dr. Thurman should do what he says he's going to do. I can't believe he did this to me. If his schedule was full, why did he say yes in the first place? Oh, well, I'm too much of a mother and a fixer, anyhow. I should never have asked if he could see my daughter. I need Dr. Thurman's approval, but I always make such a fool of myself in front of him.

C—EMOTIONAL RESPONSE: I really feel stupid because Dr. Thurman won't see my daughter. I'm sure he thinks I'm being silly about all of this, which makes me feel like I'm not worth anything. I've been humiliated, and I'm really angry.

D—TRUTHFUL SELF-TALK: Okay, wait. Let's think about this for a minute. Dr. Thurman did tell me one thing and then did another. Even though it would be nice if he did what he said he would do, he has the right to change his mind. It's true he said yes when I asked him to see my daughter, but it's also true that his schedule is full. Why he said yes is unimportant.

I do tend to be a mother and a fixer, and I'm also a mother who is concerned about her daughter. When I asked Dr. Thurman if he would see my daughter, I was doing what I thought was right at the time. I don't always make a fool of myself. My misunderstanding Dr. Thurman does not mean that I am foolish or that I'm stupid. And if Dr. Thurman thinks I'm silly, that's okay (it's not awful or terrible). I can't control what he or anyone thinks about me. And I don't have to have his approval to think well of myself.

"That is a good example," my truth-seeking patient

said. "After I wrote all that, I was able to come to our session and face you without anger or frustration. I can't believe I'd already forgotten how I did that."

"You shouldn't forget, and you should keep right on exercising your truth-seeking abilities, just like this," I said. "You took each one of your lies and came up with the truth to dispute them. In doing so, you went from being quite angry at me and the situation to being calm and assertive in talking to me about it. That's quite different from the old you, isn't it?"

"Oh, yes," she admitted. "The old me not only would have gotten very hurt and angry about the incident, but would have stayed that way. I might not have even come back to therapy, or I'd have stuffed the anger without letting you know what happened. But this time, I was able to talk myself back to the truth and deal with the event okay."

She smiled. "I'm glad you kept that journal entry," she said. "That did work for me. I'll be using that way of coping again."

I have witnessed literally hundreds of examples of improvement just like my truth-seeking patient. I wish I could show you "before" and "after" psychological and spiritual "snapshots" of many of my patients who have dedicated themselves to the truth. The "before" pictures would reveal depressed, anxious, angry, guilt-ridden people. The "after" pictures would show people who are now facing life with much less emotional baggage to weigh them down. The changes are not due to my expertise as a therapist, but are the result of the fact that anyone who dedicates his or her life to the truth will grow emotionally.

PHASE FIVE—FREEDOM TO BE OURSELVES

So now you and my truth-seeking patient know the changes that pursuit of the truth brings. There's another phase, though, embodied in a question you will sooner or later ask yourself: "After I've worked so hard to get to it, what does the truth really do for me?"

Engraved on the front of the administration building at the University of Texas are the words: "Ye shall know the truth and the truth shall set you free." While a student there, I looked at those words hundreds of times in my trips across the campus. I'm sure I believed those words. I certainly had read them in the Bible; but at a much deeper level, I am not so sure I *really* believed that they were true. In fact, during emotionally and spiritually difficult times there, those words felt totally untrue. The truth actually felt as if it was enslaving me, not setting me free.

For most of my patients, the same problem exists in their personal lives. They "mentally" believe that the truth is able to set them free. They seek counseling because they see it as a place where the truth about who they are and how they can cope better with life can be found. But for many of them, truth, once it is found, seems to hurt more than it helps. That's a major reason many patients drop out of therapy somewhere along the way. Yet as I've said so many times in these pages, the road to spiritual and emotional health is through gazing open-eyed at the truth in our lives—and the result is freedom to be what we were meant to be.

What kind of freedom is that? If you've read this far, you know I don't believe it's a freedom from pain. Pain is part of life no matter how truthfully we see ourselves, others, and the world around us. But the truth does set us free from *unnecessary pain*. Getting rid of lies is getting rid of unnecessary pain. Truth, when it does cause pain, generates constructive emotional and spiritual pain, while lies generate pain that sabotages personal growth. A life that is based on a mixture of truth and lies, which is the life most of us know, has both constructive and destructive kinds of pain.

In chapter 1, we discussed the tapes we have in our heads—the ones that continually play either truth or lies that affect our every action and thought. Take that one step further, and think of those tapes as large computer reels—computer programs, if you will. When your program is faulty because of the lies in it, the daily "data" it analyzes will trigger the wrong responses. If your program is error-free, truthful, it will call up the appropriate responses to whatever comes your way.

Has there ever been anyone who has had a totally error-free "program"? Jesus Christ was the only one. He had no "glitches" in his thinking that caused him to mis-analyze the "data" in his life. I believe that's why he could remain emotionally and spiritually healthy in the face of the horrible things that happened to him. The Bible encourages Christians to develop the "mind of Christ" for that very reason—so we too can properly handle whatever life throws at us and be healthy people. That health allows us to be "light" and "salt" to the darkness around us.

So will the truth set you free? I can tell you what I know to have been true in my life and in my patient's lives. My truth-seeking patient could tell you what she's learned. I've shown you how to go about getting rid of your lies and replacing them with the truth. But, until you've committed yourself to practicing truth, though, you'll never know what it can accomplish in your life.

In reading this far you've already made a courageous and disciplined effort to face the lies in your life and find out how the truth will help you fight them. From here, you'll make further decisions—to stay with this process or abandon it. Stay with it, no matter how long it takes. The spiritual and emotional payoffs will be there—God wired us up that way.

APPENDICES

APPENDIX A

Secular and Theological Truths for Defeating Lies

In this appendix, I list all the lies discussed in the previous chapters and the truth, both secular and theological when possible, that can be used to challenge and replace them. The different truths listed are good memory and meditation verses in your war against the lies you believe.

SELF-LIES

LIE #1: "I Must Be Perfect."

Secular Truth: To err is human.
Theological Truth: Romans 3:21–23: This righteousness from God comes through faith in Jesus Christ to all who believe. There is no difference, for all have sinned and fall short of the glory of God. **1 John 1:8:** If we claim to be without sin, we deceive ourselves and the truth is not in us.

LIE #2: "I Must Have Everyone's Love and Approval."

Secular Truth: You can't please all of the people all of the time.
Theological Truth: Colossians 3:23–24: Whatever you do, work at it with all your heart, as working for the Lord, not for men, since you know that you will receive an inheritance from the Lord as a reward. **Galatians 1:10:** Am I now trying to win the approval of men or of God? Or am I trying to please men? If I were still trying to please men, I would not be a servant of Christ.

191

LIE #3: "It Is Easier to Avoid Problems Than to Face Them."

Secular Truth: Problems usually get worse when avoided.

Theological Truth: Phillipians 3:13–14: Brothers, I do not consider myself yet to have taken hold of it. But one thing I do: Forgetting what is behind and straining toward what is ahead I press on toward the goal to win the prize for which God has called me heavenward in Christ Jesus.

LIE #4: "I Can't Be Happy Unless Things Go My Way."

Secular Truth: It isn't what happens to you that makes you unhappy, it's how you view it. So even when things don't go your way, you can still be "happy" (content) with the proper attitude.

Theological Truth: Acts 20:22–24: And now, compelled by the Spirit, I am going to Jerusalem, not knowing what will happen to me there. I only know that in every city the Holy Spirit warns me that prison and hardships are facing me. However, I consider my life worth nothing to me, if only I may finish the race and complete the task the Lord Jesus has given me—the task of testifying to the gospel of God's grace. **Philippians 4:11–13:** I am not saying this because I am in need, for I have learned to be content whatever the circumstances. I know what it is to be in need, and I know what it is to have plenty. I have learned the secret of being content in any and every situation, whether well fed or hungry, whether living in plenty or want. I can do everything through him who gives me strength. **James 1:2–3:** Consider it pure joy, my brothers, whenever you face trials, because you know that the testing of your faith develops perseverance.

LIE #5: "It's Somebody Else's Fault."

Secular Truth: Our feelings, whether pleasant or unpleasant, are caused by how we think. Since no one forces us to think the way we choose to think, we are responsible for the feelings that our thoughts create. Our unhappiness (or happiness) is our "fault."

Theological Truth: Proverbs 23:7: As [a man] thinks in his heart, so is he.

WORLDLY LIES

LIE #1: "You Can Have It All."

Secular Truth: No one really has it all. Everyone has gaps in his or her life.
Theological Truth: 1 John 2:15–17: Do not love the world or anything in the world. If anyone loves the world, the love of the Father is not in him. For everything in the world—the cravings of sinful man, the lust of his eyes, and the boasting of what he has and does—comes not from the Father but from the world. The world and its desires pass away, but the man who does the will of God lives forever. **1 Timothy 6:7–10:** For we brought nothing into the world, and we can take nothing out of it. But if we have food and clothing, we will be content with that. People who want to get rich fall into temptation and a trap and into many foolish and harmful desires that plunge men into ruin and destruction. "For the love of money is a root of all kinds of evil." Some people, eager for money, have wandered from the faith and pierced themselves with many griefs.

LIE #2: "You Are Only as Good as What You Do."

Secular Truth: Your worth is tied to who you are, not what you do.
Theological Truth: Galatians 3:10–11: All who rely on the law are under a curse, for it is written: "Cursed is everyone who does not continue to do everything written in the Book of the Law." Clearly no one is justified before God by the law because, "The righteous will live by faith."

LIE #3: "Life Should Be Easy."

Secular Truth: Life is rough. A great deal of hardship and frustration is built into it.
Theological Truth: John 16:33: I have told you these things so that in me you may have peace. In this world you will have trouble. But take heart! I have overcome the world.

LIE #3: "Life Should Be Fair."

Secular Truth: Life is sometimes fair and sometimes unfair.
Theological Truth: Ecclesiastes 8:14: Something else mean-

ingless occurs on earth: righteous men who get what the wicked deserve, and wicked men who get what the righteous deserve. This too, I say, is meaningless.

LIE #4: "Don't Wait."

Secular Truth: Patience is a virtue. It is often healthier to delay gratification rather than seek immediate gratification.
Theological Truth: Galatians 6:7–8: "Do not be deceived, God is not mocked." A man reaps what he sows. The one who sows to please his sinful nature will reap destruction; the one who sows to please the Spirit, from the Spirit will reap eternal life. **Proverbs 14:29:** A patient man has great understanding, but a quick-tempered man displays folly.

LIE #5: "People Are Basically Good."

Secular Truth: People have both good and evil inside of them, and they seem as bent on self-destruction as they do on growth.
Theological Truth: Jeremiah 17:9: "The heart is deceitful above all things" and beyond cure. Who can understand it? **Matthew 15:19:** For out of the heart come evil thoughts, murder, adultery, sexual immorality, theft, false testimony, slander. **Romans 3:10–12:** As it is written: "There is no one righteous, not even one; there is none who understands, none who seeks God. All have turned away, they have together become worthless, there is no one who does good, not even one." **Galatians 5:19:** The acts of the sinful nature are obvious: sexual immorality, impurity and debauchery; idolatry and witchcraft; hatred, discord, jealousy, fits of rage, selfish ambition, dissensions, factions, and envy; drunkenness, orgies, and the like.

MARITAL LIES

LIE #1: "It's All Your Fault."

Secular Truth: It takes two to tango. Marriage problems are rarely one person's fault.
Theological Truth: Romans 2:1: You, therefore, have no excuse, you who pass judgment on someone else, for at whatever point you judge the other, you are condemning yourself, because you who pass judgment do the same things.

LIE #2: "If It Takes Hard Work, We Must Not Be Right for Each Other."

Secular Truth: Hard work in marriage is the norm, not the exception. It means you and your partner need each other's help to work out personality flaws and weaknesses.

Theological Truth: 1 Corinthians 7:28b: But those who marry will face many troubles in this life.

LIE #3: "You Can and Should Meet All My Needs."

Secular Truth: No one person can meet all your needs. Your needs can best be met through a variety of sources.

Theological Truth: Philippians 4:19: And my God will meet all your needs according to his glorious riches in Christ Jesus.

LIE #4: "You Owe Me."

Secular Truth: Your spouse doesn't really "owe" you anything for what you do. You do what you do because, at some level, you choose to do it. You aren't owed anything for what you choose to do.

Theological Truth: 1 Peter 5:5b: Clothe yourselves with humility because "God resists the proud, but gives grace to the humble."

LIE #5: "I Shouldn't Have to Change."

Secular Truth: Marriage requires change. People who refuse to change stagnate themselves and their marriages. The important issue is deciding what we need to change about ourselves and what we don't.

Theological Truth: Hebrews 12:14a: Make every effort to live in peace with all and to be holy.

LIE #6: "You Should Be Like Me."

Secular Truth: Every person is unique and can't be a carbon copy of anyone else. It would be boring if it weren't that way.

Theological Truth: 1 Corinthians 12:18–19: But in fact God has arranged the parts in the body, every one of them, just as he wanted them to be. If they were all one part, where would the body be?

DISTORTION LIES

LIE #1: Magnification

Secular Truth: Mountains are not molehills. Five-dollar events are five-dollar events, not fifty-dollar events.

LIE #2: Personalization

Secular Truth: We are not the target or cause of everything that happens to us. Many life events that happen directly to us are not meant personally and are more a statement about the person who did them than about us.

LIE #3: Polarization

Secular Truth: While some issues in life are black/white, many issues are some shade of grey. Black/white issues need to be seen as black or white, but issues that are grey need to be seen that way.

LIE #4: Selective Abstraction

Secular Truth: While we often have to focus on a specific "tree" in life, we need to keep the whole "forest" in mind. No matter what parts there are to focus on, we need to see the whole.

LIE #5: Overgeneralization

Secular Truth: What happens to us in the "here and now" is not necessarily what has to happen again to us in the future. History doesn't have to repeat itself.

LIE #6: Emotional Reasoning

Secular Truth: Feelings aren't facts; feelings are feelings.

RELIGIOUS LIES

LIE #1: "God's Love Must Be Earned."

Theological Truth: Romans 5:8: But God demonstrates his own love toward us, in that: while we were still sinners, Christ died for us. **Ephesians 2:8–9:** "For by grace you have been saved through faith, and that not of yourselves; it is the gift of God, not of works," so that no one can boast.

LIE #2: "God Hates the Sin and the Sinner."

Theological Truth: John 8:11: The woman caught in adultery. **Romans 5:8:** "But God demonstrates his own love toward us, in that: while we were still sinners, Christ died for us."

LIE #3: "Because I'm a Christian, God Will Protect Me from Pain and Suffering."

Theological Truth: 1 Peter 4:12–13: Dear friends, do not be surprised at the painful trial you are suffering, as though something strange were happening to you. But rejoice that you participate in the suffering of Christ, so that you may be overjoyed when his glory is revealed. **John 16:33:** I have told you these things so "that in me you may have peace." In this world you will have trouble. But take heart! I have overcome the world. **Philippians 1:29:** For it has been granted to you on behalf of Christ not only to believe on him, but also to suffer for him.

LIE #4: "All My Problems Are Caused by My Sins."

Theological Truth: John 9:1–3: As he went along, he saw a man blind from birth. His disciples asked him, "Rabbi, who sinned, this man or his parents, that he was born blind?" "Neither this man nor his parents sinned," said Jesus, "but [this happened so] that the work of God might be revealed in his life."

LIE #5: "It Is My Christian Duty to Meet All the Needs of Others."

Theological Truth: 1 Corinthians 12:27–31: Now you are the body of Christ, and each of you is a part of it. And in the church God has appointed first of all apostles, second prophets, third teachers, then workers of miracles, also those having gifts of healing, those able to help others, those with gifts of administration, and those speaking in different kinds of tongues. Are all apostles? Are all prophets? Are all teachers? Do all work miracles? Do all have gifts of healing? Do all speak in tongues? Do all interpret? But eagerly desire the greater gifts. **Romans 12:6–7:** We have different gifts, according to the grace given us. If a man's gift is prophesying, let him use it in proportion to his faith. If it is serving, let him serve; if teaching, let him teach; if encouraging, let him encourage; if contributing to the needs of others, let him give generously; if leadership, let him govern diligently; if showing mercy, let him do it cheerfully.

LIE #6: "A Good Christian Doesn't Feel Angry, Anxious or Depressed."

Theological Truth: John 11:33–35: When Jesus saw her weeping and the Jews who had come along with her also weeping, he was deeply moved and troubled. "Where have you laid him?" he asked. "Lord, come and see," they replied. Jesus wept. **Mark 14:32–34:** They went to a place called Gethsemane, and Jesus said to his disciples, "Sit here while I pray." He took Peter, James, and John along, and he began to be deeply distressed and troubled. "My soul is overwhelmed with sorrow to the point of death," he said to them. "Stay here and keep watch." **Mark 11:15–16:** On reaching Jerusalem, Jesus entered the temple area and began driving out those who were buying and selling there. He overturned the tables of the moneychangers and the benches of those selling doves, and would not allow anyone to carry merchandise through the temple courts. **Ephesians 4:26:** In your anger, do not sin.

LIE #7: "God Can't Use Me Unless I'm Spiritually Strong."

Theological Truth: 2 Corinthians 13:4: For to be sure, he was crucified in weakness, yet he lives by God's power. Likewise, we are weak in him, yet by God's power we will live with him to serve you. **2 Corinthians 12:9–10:** But he said to me, "My grace is sufficient for you, for My strength is made perfect in weakness." Therefore, I will boast all the more gladly about my weaknesses, so that Christ's power may rest on me. That is why, for Christ's sake, I delight in weaknesses, in insults, in hardships, in persecution, in difficulties. For when I am weak, then I am strong. **1 Corinthians 1:27:** But God chose the foolish things of the world to shame the wise; God chose the weak things of the world to shame the strong. **1 Corinthians 9:22:** To the weak I became weak to win the weak.

APPENDIX B

Secular and Theological Teachings on the Importance of the Mind for Healthy Living

SECULAR TEACHINGS

Epictetus: "Man is disturbed not by things but by the view he takes of them."

William Shakespeare: "There is nothing either good nor bad but thinking makes it so."

Benedict (Baruch) Spinoza: "I saw that all the things I feared, and which feared me, had nothing good or bad in them insofar as the mind was affected by them."

Marcus Aurelius: "If you are pained by an external thing, it is not the thing that disturbs you, but your own judgment about it. And it is in your power to wipe out this judgment now."

Immanuel Kant: "The only feature common to all mental disorders is the loss of common sense and the compensatory development of a unique private sense of reasoning."

W. E. B. DuBois: "If we wish to change the sentiments it is necessary before all to modify the idea which produced them, and to recognize either that it is not correct itself, or that it does not touch our interests."

199

Alfred Adler: "It is very obvious that we are influenced not by 'facts' but by our interpretation of facts."

John Milton: "The mind is its own place, and in itself/Can make a heaven of Hell, a hell of Heaven."

I. E. Farber: "The one thing psychologists can count on is that their subjects will talk if only to themselves; and not infrequently, whether relevant or irrelevant, the things people say to themselves determine the rest of the things they do.

THEOLOGICAL TEACHINGS

Proverbs 23:7: For as [a man] thinketh in his heart, so is he.

Philippians 2:5: Your attitude should be the same as that of Christ Jesus.

Romans 12:2: Do not conform any longer to the pattern of this world, but be transformed by the renewing of your mind. Then you will be able to test and approve what God's will is—his good, pleasing and perfect will.

Philippians 4:8: Finally, brothers, whatever is true, whatever is noble, whatever is right, whatever is pure, whatever is lovely, whatever is admirable—if anything is excellent or praiseworthy, think about such things.

Romans 1:28: Furthermore, since they did not think it worthwhile to retain the knowledge of God, he gave them over to a depraved mind, to do what ought not to be done.

Romans 8:6–7: The mind of sinful man is death, but the mind controlled by the Spirit is life and peace; the sinful mind is hostile to God. It does not submit to God's law, nor can it do so.

Ephesians 4:22: You were taught, with regard to your former way of life, to put off the old self, which is being corrupted by its deceitful desires; to be made new in the attitude of your minds, and to put on the new self, created to be like God in true righteousness and holiness.

Colossians 3:2: Set your minds on things above, not on earthly things.

2 Corinthians 10:5: We demolish arguments and every pretension that sets itself up against the knowledge of God, and we take captive every thought and make it obedient to Christ.

Isaiah 26:3: You will keep him in perfect peace whose mind is steadfast, because he trusts you.

Proverbs 14:15: A simple man believes anything, but a prudent man gives thought to his steps.

APPENDIX C

Reading List

Allen, James. *As a Man Thinketh*. Fort Worth, TX: Brownlow, 1985.

Backus, William, and Marie Chapian. *Telling Yourself the Truth*. Minneapolis, MN: Bethany House, 1980.

Burns, David D. *Feeling Good: The New Mood Therapy*. New York: Signet, 1981.

Ellis, Albert, and Robert A. Harper. *A New Guide To Rational Living*. North Hollywood, CA: Wilshire, 1975.

Powell, John. *Fully Human, Fully Alive*. Valencia, CA: Tabor Pub., 1976.

Stoop, David. *Self Talk: Key to Personal Growth*. Old Tappan, NJ: Revell, 1981.

Woodbridge, John, ed. *Renewing Your Mind in a Secular World*. Chicago: Moody, 1985.

NOTES

Chapter 1
1. James Allen, *As a Man Thinketh* (Ft. Worth, TX: Brownlow Publishing Co., 1985), 20.

Chapter 2
1. David Burns, "The Perfectionist's Script for Self-Defeat," *Psychology Today,* Nov. 1980, 34.
2. M. Scott Peck, *The Road Less Traveled: A New Psychology of Love, Traditional Values and Spiritual Growth* (New York: Simon and Schuster, 1978), 16-17.

Chapter 3
1. Ecclesiastes 2:4–10.
2. Ecclesiastes 5:12.
3. Ecclesiastes 5:10.
4. Ecclesiastes 1:14.
5. 1 Timothy 6:7–8.
6. Psalms 8:5.
7. Psalms 139:14; 1 Corinthians 6:20.
8. Peck, *Road,* 15.
9. John 16:33.
10. Romans 8:28.
11. Tim Hansel, *When I Relax I Feel Guilty* (Elgin, IL: Cook, 1979).
12. Ecclesiastes 8:14.
13. Psalms 27:14; Matthew 6:19.
14. Abraham Maslow, *Toward a Psychology of Being,* 2nd ed. (New York: Van Nostrand, 1968), 3–4.
15. Galatians 5:19 (NIV).

Chapter 4
1. William J. Lederer and Don Jackson, *The Mirages of Marriage* (New York: Norton, 1968), 40.
2. Matthew 7:3.
3. 1 Corinthians 7:28 (NIV).
4. James 1:19.
5. Genesis 2:24.

Chapter 5
1. Peck, *Road*, 44.
2. David Burns, *Feeling Good: The New Mood Therapy* (New York: Signet, 1980).

Chapter 6
1. Doug Moo, "Putting the Renewed Mind to Work," *Renewing Your Mind in a Secular World*, ed. John D. Woodridge (Chicago: Moody, 1985), 145.
2. Ephesians 2:8.
3. 2 Timothy 1:9.
4. Romans 5:8.
5. John 8:7.
6. John 8:11.
7. John 9:1–3.
8. Romans 8:28 (NIV).
9. Matthew 11:28-30.
10. Luke 10:41–42.
11. Matthew 26:38 (NIV).
12. 2 Corinthians 12:10.
13. Matthew 9:12.
14. John 8:44.
15. Philippians 4:7.
16. Romans 3:23.

Chapter 7
1. 2 Timothy 3:16–17.
2. Peck, *Road*, 44.
3. Proverbs 23:7.
4. John 20:27.

About the Author

Chris Thurman is a licensed psychologist in counseling practice at the Minirth-Meier Clinic in Richardson, Texas. He holds a Ph.D. in counseling psychology from the University of Texas at Austin. Before joining the Minirth-Meier Clinic, Dr. Thurman was a psychologist in the counseling center and assistant professor in psychology at North Texas State University. He has published numerous articles on stress, anger, and Type A (coronary-prone) behavior in leading psychological journals. Dr. Thurman appears frequently on national radio and television talk programs. He and his wife, Holly, have two children, Matthew and Ashley.

NOTES

NOTES

NOTES

NOTES

NOTES

NOTES

NOTES

NOTES

NOTES

NOTES

NOTES